Christians are to  in a broken world. Yet, we ourselves are
Briggs inspires us and guides us in the recovery of our Christ-shaped calling to be wounded healers. Biblically grounded and pastorally urgent, this is a charge for the church today.

Rev. Dr. Glenn Packiam
Associate Senior Pastor, New Life Church
Author of *Blessed Broken Given*

With the pandemic, recent natural disasters, and continuing political unrest, *A Time to Heal* is a timely book which offers encouragement, healing, and hope for those of us who lead in times of chaos and serve a hurting world in Jesus' name. J.R. Briggs has done an outstanding job of synthesizing biblical principles, research, and personal stories. It's a book I highly recommend for churches, study groups, or individuals.

Jamie Aten, Ph.D.
Founder & Co-Director
Humanitarian Disaster Institute at Wheaton College

In these times of injustice, brokenness and pandemic, the world is looking for healers. In this fine book, J.R. Briggs asks, "Can Christians be His presence in the midst of suffering and lead the world to healing?" With Scriptural direction, insightful observations, and personal testimony, he illuminates the way of "the Wounded Healer." *A Time to Heal* is for all of us who long to be the people the world is looking for.

David Fitch, Ph.D.
Professor of Theology, Northern Seminary
Author of *Faithful Presence*

J.R. Briggs is a perceptive and trustworthy guide to the exhilarating – albeit sometimes terrifying – experience of living in the kingdom of God. This book provides helpful encouragement for Jesus followers seeking to live faithfully in the reality of God's healing action for this unique moment in time.

Dr. Susan Billington Harper
Managing Director of Church Advancement,
American Bible Society

The world is emerging from perhaps its most painful season in modern memory. The question before all the people of God is "will there be a church there to meet them?" In *A Time to Heal* we meet with both a fresh reminder of the true calling for followers of Jesus in the world and practical steps to guide us along the way. There couldn't be a more timely book!

Dr. Chris Backert
National Director of Fresh Expressions US

A **FRESH EXPRESSIONS** BOOK

A TIME TO HEAL

OFFERING HOPE to a WOUNDED WORLD in the NAME of JESUS

J.R. BRIGGS

Copyright © 2021 J.R. Briggs

All rights reserved. No part of this publication may be reproduced, distributed or transmitted in any form or by any means, including photo- copying, recording, or other electronic or mechanical methods, without the prior written permission of the publisher, except in the case of brief quotations embodied in critical reviews and certain other noncommercial uses permitted by copyright law.

Unless otherwise indicated, all Scriptures are quoted from THE HOLY BIBLE, NEW INTERNATIONAL VERSION®, NIV® Copyright © 1973, 1978, 1984, 2011 by Biblica, Inc.™ Used by permission. All rights reserved worldwide.

Scriptures marked NET are from the NET Bible® copyright ©1996-2006 by Biblical Studies Press, L.L.C. http://netbible.com All rights reserved.

Scriptures marked NLT are from the *Holy Bible*, New Living Translation, copyright © 1996, 2004, 2015 by Tyndale House Foundation. Used by permission of Tyndale House Publishers, Inc., Carol Stream, Illinois 60188. All rights reserved.

For permission requests, write to the publisher, addressed "Attention: Permissions Coordinator," at the address below.

Published by: HigherLife Publishing & Marketing
  PO Box 623307
  Oviedo, FL 32762
  AHigherLife.com

A Time to Heal: Offering Hope to a Wounded World in the Name of Jesus -- 1st ed.

ISBN 978-1-954533-03-5 Paperback

Library of Congress Number: 2021901157

Printed in the United States of America.

10 9 8 7 6 5 4 3 2 1

Also by J.R. Briggs

Books

The Sacred Overlap

Fail

Eldership and the Mission of God (with Bob Hyatt)

Ministry Mantras (with Bob Hyatt)

Why Ask Questions? (with Michael Smith)

Contributions

The Abide Bible

The Message Remix: Solo

To Matt Lake

For our friendship. And our hikes.

Contents

Preface xiii

1 What Do We Do with Our Wounds? 1

2 What Is the Hope We Have – and Have to Offer? 13

3 How Did Jesus Heal — and How Are We to Join Him in the Healing Process? 27

4 How Will the Church Be the Body of Christ to a Hurting World? 39

5 How Can We Deepen Our Trust in the Holy Spirit to Guide Us as Healers? 63

6 How Can We Be Prepared to Be Bringers of Healing? 75

7 What Are the Marks of Wounded Healers? 85

8 What Is the Connection Between Leadership and Healing? 99

Conclusion: The Importance of Connection 107

Acknowledgments 109

Recommended Resources 113

Endnotes 117

*Surely he took up our pain
  and bore our suffering,
yet we considered him punished by God,
  stricken by him, and afflicted.
But he was pierced for our transgressions,
  he was crushed for our iniquities;
the punishment that brought us peace was on him,
  and by his wounds we are healed.*
  —ISAIAH 53:4-5 (NIV)

*Christ has no body but yours,
No hands, no feet on earth but yours,
Yours are the eyes with which he looks
Compassion on this world,
Yours are the feet with which he walks to do good,
Yours are the hands, with which he blesses all the
 world.
Yours are the hands, yours are the feet,
Yours are the eyes, you are his body.
Christ has no body now on earth but yours.*
  —SAINT TERESA OF AVILA (1515-1582)

Preface

When the novel COVID-19 coronavirus invaded the U.S. in the early months of 2020 and spread with woeful consequence in the months thereafter, it ushered in uncertainty, pain, and loss. For some, this loss was acute and devastating. For others, it presented as an omnipresent undercurrent of anxiety and malaise. And for others, still, it became a lightning rod of frustration and division. Yet even before the virus struck the U.S., our country was already experiencing a bevy of change, division, and uncertainty, both inside and outside the Church.

In the early phase of the pernicious pandemic, as we were beginning to grasp the long-term implications the virus would have on our world, my friend Dr. Leonard Sweet offered how the Church was called in the moment to join God in the healing process. I was seized by this thought. I couldn't shake the unbelievably ripe opportunity available to God's people – the opportunity to serve those who were lonely, anxious, wounded, and traumatized, who were in need of the hope and healing found in Christ.

I, like many in the spring of 2020, struggled to find adequate rest. It was almost four months into the pandemic before I experienced my first decent night's sleep. But my restless nights were not a result of worry or fear. While I was burdened by the omnipresent pain and uncertainty I observed in my neighborhood and around the world, the reason behind my sleeplessness was due largely to the fact that I couldn't turn off my mind. It raced and whirled as I pondered Len's words and contemplated the myriad implications for the Church in this cultural moment. These implications initiated a barrage of ideas, questions, possibilities, and creative opportunities.

Each night, as my family headed to bed, it was as if I was just waking up. Just before midnight, the fuses of my mental rockets were lit and began exploding. One of those mental rockets became the vision of this book. I would ascend to my office on the top floor of our home and write for two – sometimes three – hours until I had dumped everything from my mind onto the paper; when my brain was empty, I'd fall into bed. In that stretch of time, I was physically exhausted, yet mentally exhilarated. Writing a book is most often a long, slow, and arduous process, taking months – sometimes years – to complete. But the vast majority of this book coalesced in just five weeks' time. Certainly, there were tweaks, edits, changes, and re-writes in the months thereafter, but the majority of the content grabbed me by the throat in those few weeks and refused to let go. It came to me with a sense of clarity and urgency I hadn't experienced before as a writer.

The book you hold in your hands is not about the novel coronavirus specifically. However, the world-altering reality of the pandemic and its global implications paved the way for us to see with sharp clarity the reality of our collective woundedness and the ripe opportunity to partner with God as bearers of healing. This hopeful, redemptive invitation became the lens through which I began to study the Scriptures, pray, reflect, converse, and teach. It still is. I imagine it will for years to come. I hope the message of this book grips you in much the same way it has gripped me.

J.R. Briggs
March 2021

Chapter 1

What Do We Do with Our Wounds?

There are many, many wounded! So many people need their wounds healed! This is the mission of the Church: to heal the wounds of the heart, to open doors, to free people.[1]
—POPE FRANCIS

It is not the healthy who need a doctor, but the sick.
—JESUS, LUKE 5:31

About an hour ago I received the call that Chip died. As I type these words, the tears are still warm on my cheeks. Over the past few years, Chip was a regular participant at our church. He'd lived a difficult life, and his health had been in significant decline. For the past few years, a dialysis machine kept him alive three days a week. Chip was not infected by the virus, although he was deeply affected by it. The complexity of life, disconnection from his community due to the lockdown, and a harrowing feeling overwhelmed him so much that he wondered if dialysis was still worth the effort.

When I called to check in on him around lunchtime, he explained he was going to stop his dialysis treatments altogether. He knew if he ended his treatments he would most likely die within a few days, but he told me he was at peace with his decision. As we spoke on the phone, his breathing was noticeably labored. Between gasps of air, he shared that he refused to be admitted to the hospital because visitors were not allowed due to restrictions and he feared he would die alone. When I hung up the phone, I wondered if that was the last time I would speak to Chip. That afternoon, after discussing the options with his home visit nurse, a family member, and one of our pastors, he finally agreed to be admitted. As paramedics arrived in his living room to transport him to the hospital, he went into cardiac arrest. Chip died, but not alone.

Hundreds of thousands have died because of the virus, either directly from contracting it, or indirectly like Chip. Over the years, our church loved Chip well. The number of sacrificial acts of love, service, and kindness extended to him was inspiring, and thus, his loss was difficult for our community. Due to the lockdown mandate in the spring of 2020, we were forced to attend Chip's memorial service on Zoom. How are we to appropriately grieve the passing of our friend and comfort his family and one another through a glowing rectangular screen?

Our Wounding Reality

While the pandemic impacted Chip and those who loved him, it has, of course, impacted everyone on the globe at some level or another. In December 2020, the U.S. Food and Drug Administration formally approved two vaccines and began its global rollout just before Christmas. The vaccine provided hope, in what many declared as a light at the end of the tunnel. Hopeful as the news of the vaccines were, it won't – and can't – fix the damage that has been done to the world in this pandemic. It can prevent the virus from getting worse and help to bring an eventual end to this global nightmare, but people of compassion are needed in this season to help the world heal from the damage we experienced in the wake of this virus. And this healing will take years.

The Associated Press reported there were over 3 million deaths in the U.S. in 2020, the deadliest year ever recorded in our history.[2] At the time of this writing, 2.7 million people around the world have died from the virus, just under 535,000 in the United States alone – 178 times greater than who died from 9/11 and far more American deaths than were lost in the Vietnam, Korean, and Persian Gulf Wars combined. The virus took more lives in one year than in the entirety of World War II. We have all experienced its wounding effects in our lives, our relationships, our finances, our spiritual lives, and even our thinking. Even before the virus arrived on our shores, we were in the midst of the deadliest drug overdose epidemic in U.S. history. The pandemic made things worse, accounting for the most overdose deaths ever recorded.[3] Sadly, the vulnerable were impacted disproportionately by these global events. Economists commonly use the phrase "disasters punch down" – crises significantly impact the elderly, the sick, the poor, and, quite often, people of color. Those who were already struggling before these mounting crises felt the punches even more in the midst of them.

There may not always be acute healing that's needed. There may not even be pervasive and evident chronic healing needed either. It may evidence itself in a much subtler expression: restlessness, meaninglessness, loneliness, purposelessness, and boredom. Our modern culture is built around the gods of accumulation and accomplishment. Many have been wounded by these promises the gods offered but were never able to fulfill. How do we help people heal from this deep disappointment? We may not have tested positive for the virus, but we were all affected, directly or indirectly.

2020 took its toll on us.

In January, wildfires raged in Australia, and the World Health Organization confirmed cases of the COVID-19 coronavirus.

In March and April, many states went into lockdown, with

only essential locations remaining open. The Dow Jones recorded its worst point drops since the Great Depression. Many felt too anxious to be productive, too restless to sleep well, too depressed to be able to sit quietly with our thoughts, and too exhausted to do much of anything at all. High school and college seniors did not get a chance to walk at their graduations. Weddings were altered; funerals were postponed or pushed online.[4]

During the spring lockdown, the federal domestic abuse hotline experienced almost a 900 percent increase in volume.[5] One British study of domestic violence found more women were killed by men in the U.K. during the first three weeks of the lockdown than at any three-week period of time in its country's history.[6]

COVID-19 wasn't the only thing that spread. During the last week of May, horrific videos of unjust and unnecessary killings of black Americans surfaced. At the time of this writing, the deaths of Ahmaud Arbery and Breonna Taylor, among many others, were fresh on our minds. The following week was punctuated by yet another death: George Floyd. First, the global spread and uncertainty around the virus; then the video of a Minneapolis police officer kneeling on Floyd's neck for almost nine minutes went viral. Peaceful protests arose across cities; some protests fulminated, which led to rioting, setting communities aflame and even more death —all in the same week the U.S. registered 100,000 deaths from the virus.

By July, forty-eight million Americans had filed for unemployment. In late summer and early fall, while hurricanes and trouble storms hit the southeastern parts of the U.S., wildfires in the American west unleashed unimaginable damage. California, Oregon, and Washington were dealing with new and troubling levels of uncertainty once again, with thousands of residents displaced.

In the fall, many states throughout the U.S. experienced a

surge in cases, hospitalizations, and deaths. Many families chose not to spend time with loved ones during the Thanksgiving and Christmas holidays.

Few spaces of our world have been left untouched by the unrelenting waves of crises we've experienced. It was Lenin who famously uttered, "There are decades where nothing happens; and there are weeks where decades happen." Within a few weeks' time, we felt that decades' worth of impact.

The health sector experienced immense stress. Hospitals were strained. Nursing homes and assisted living facilities were decimated. Refrigerated trucks were parked outside of hospitals in cities such as New York City and El Paso because morgues were past capacity.

Education was disrupted, with distance learning for millions of children and their families for months. Most colleges and universities kept students home for the spring semester. When many students returned in the fall, confirmed cases spiked and were then kept on campus so as not to send them back home to spread the virus even further. Buckling under the economic stress, some colleges and universities closed for good.

The economy was vulnerable and erratic. Millions of Americans lost jobs – either temporarily or permanently – as the government intervened to provide Americans with more than one round of stimulus checks to keep the economy afloat. For many people, the money ran out much too quickly. Businesses, large and small, were upended economically; many were shuttered.

The entertainment industry was hit hard – from the film industry, to musicians and other artists who were used to performing in crowded venues. Amateur and professional sports schedules were postponed, and seasons cancelled. NBA star Karl-Anthony Towns of the Minnesota Timberwolves lost his mother *and six other relatives* due to complications of COVID-19. He was later diagnosed with the virus in January 2021.[7]

The prison system was significantly disrupted. Many non-violent offenders were sent home to mitigate the spread in overcrowded correctional facilities.

Churches were forced to close their (physical) doors, and services were moved to online platforms, leaving people feeling spiritually homeless, isolated, and disconnected.

Mental health issues spiked with a dramatic increase across the country and around the world. As isolation and national anxiety rose, social connection all but disappeared for months, creating a dangerous combination for those already feeling emotionally vulnerable.

Some of the world's top political leaders contracted the virus, including Boris Johnson in the U.K., Emmanuel Macron of France, Jair Bolsonaro of Brazil, and in the U.S. with Donald Trump and his wife Melania. Other American governors and members of Congress tested positive. Ambrose Dlamini, the Prime Minister of Eswatini (formerly Swaziland) died after testing positive.

Even our social interactions changed, as hugs and handshakes were replaced with social distancing and waving with masks on. Masks became a source of immense scrutiny, division, and anger, causing further pain and woundedness.

BibleGateway.com and the Bible app YouVersion reported a record number of people searched for *healing, fear*, and *justice* in 2020. YouVersion reported an 80% increase in searches, with Isaiah 41:10 as the most read, searched, and bookmarked verse: "So do not fear, for I am with you; do not be dismayed, for I am your God. I will strengthen you and help you; I will uphold you with my righteous right hand."[8]

But the calamity didn't stop at year's end. 2021 began with spiking virus cases and a politically splintered country, with many claiming Joe Biden had stolen the U.S. presidential election away from Donald Trump. This sentiment reached its climax on January 6, 2021, as a violent mob of Trump supporters breached security perimeters and stormed the U.S. Capitol building in an effort to thwart the certification process of Joe Biden's victory. The supporters rioted, confronted police, and vandalized one of America's most revered buildings.[9] In the midst of the violence inside the Capitol, five people were killed, including one police officer. Trump's incitement of violence among his most ardent followers led members of Congress to vote for his impeachment once again, making him the first president in American history to be impeached twice. In the aftermath, and in preparation for the U.S. presidential inauguration, the Pentagon authorized the mobilization of 25,000 National Guard members. They were tasked with keeping the peace, providing safety, and ensuring security during the transfer of power in every state and the District of Columbia.

On January 19, 2021, on the eve of the presidential inauguration, the Washington National Cathedral funeral bell tolled 400 times – one for every 1,000 people who had died from the virus. At that same hour, President-elect Joe Biden and Vice President-elect Kamala Harris, along with their spouses, attended a quiet and somber ceremony at the Lincoln Memorial in Washington D.C. with 400 illumined fixtures lining the edge of the Reflecting Pool. Cities around the nation shared in the memorial, as churches and government buildings were lit to honor those who had been lost. At the ceremony Biden shared, "It's hard sometimes to remember, but that's how we heal."[10]

And on January 20, 2021, in his inauguration speech Biden stated, "We'll press forward with speed and urgency for we have much to do in this winter of peril and significant possibility. Much to do, much to heal, much to restore, much to build, and much to gain." Biden assumed the mantle of responsibility at a dark time when our nation was saturated with sickness, marked by death, and burdened with more political division than at any point in our lifetime.

There is no map, no compass, no trail markers, nor well-worn path to follow in tumultuous, wounding times. We are left with few tools or signposts for guidance in the midst of massive amounts of pain, loss, fear, and grief in our collective PTSD. How are we to serve and lead in the wake of such uncertain, intense, and divisive times? How can we show one another that, despite all the pain, hope is still real? How are we to lead when the whole world seems to have gone off the map?

Initially, our collective focus was on the need for *physical* healing from the virus, followed quickly by the need for *economic* and *financial* healing that ensued. Then the *emotional, mental,* and *relational* needs were pressing due to isolation, lockdown, and division. Suicide attempts, domestic abuse, and depression spiked. Following quickly on its heels, there was desperate need for *racial* healing in our country after the senseless acts of brutality recorded on people's cell phones. Numerous crises and disasters around the world and in the U.S. culminated into what many described as one large, ongoing, overwhelming, scary reality. In all of this, our *spiritual* needs become front and center. So many were hurting. So many still are. So many will be for quite some time. We are all in need of healing. The central question we'll explore is this book: *What is the role of the church in a time of such pervasive loss and deep pain – and what role will the church play in the healing process?*

The Christian motif of death and resurrection serves as a significant model for our leadership in the days ahead. In what amounted to one of the most surreal Lenten seasons and Holy Weeks of our lifetime, in 2020 we still were able to remember and celebrate Jesus, who wore a *corona* of thorns and died so we may be healed from the deadly virus of sin. It was a Lenten reflection which focused our attention on mortality in the most experiential way and left us longing for resurrection. We still long for resurrection from all of this pain.

Leading in a New Reality

Tod Bolsinger, in his book *Canoeing the Mountains,* made the bold claim: our old strategies of leadership no longer work. It is one thing to prepare for leading off the map in a rapidly changing world. It is quite another to be leading off the map in a world that had changed so rapidly.[11] Health professionals, government officials, and medical workers scrambled to secure N95 masks and other personal protective equipment (PPE), so they had the tools needed to adequately care for the sick. In many ways, this served as a poignant metaphor for what church leaders felt – and continue to feel. *How shall we lead if we are ill-equipped to fulfill our calling in the world?*

As leaders, we possess experience, we've earned degrees, and we've honed our skills. These have been helpful and served us in the past. But we've run into one glaring problem: *the world in front of us is nothing like the world behind us.* Leaders learned that in a pandemic, much of our education, expertise, and experience can reach an expiration date. A major upheaval of economic, racial, political, and social systems has occurred – and is still unfolding. Any warning signs about the future of the church in the first two decades of the twentieth century were dwarfed in proportion by the myriad cascading crises ushered forth in 2020. We have been grieving the magnitude of loss and change.[12] How shall we lead in a time like this?

Following Jesus is about joining His mission in the world. Theologian Christopher Wright wrote, "It is not so much that God has a mission for his church in the world, but that God has a church for his mission in the world."[13] And Jesus' mission was about *shalom* – the restoring, redeeming, and renewing of the world to peace, rightness and harmony. Luke records

Jesus' poignant words: *"It is not the healthy who need a doctor, but the sick"* (5:31). As Jordan Seng wrote, "In the kingdom of God, healing is the default position."[14] The church, in its global and local expressions, is to throw open its doors as a hospital of hope. In great paradox, it is this perfect, all-powerful God who graciously invites broken people like you and me to bring healing to his world. As Seng also reminds, our healing work certainly won't be perfect, but we shouldn't abandon healing or preaching ministry simply because it's hard.[15] We don't have to construct a grand vision or a complex plan; instead, we can join God's mission by looking around and noticing the pain – and moving toward it with faith, courage, and compassion. Just as God moved toward his people to restore shalom in the world, we are called to move toward the world to bring restoration and healing.

So, what should followers of Jesus do now?

And how shall we lead in this astoundingly complex off-the-map situation?

Where does one turn when no one is an expert and none of us have been here before?

Will we re-double our efforts and attempt to return to the past to the way we've always done it?

Will we shrink back, or will we boldly lean into the future?

How do we navigate a new world we were not trained for – and that nobody saw coming?

And what if the leaders of the future could only offer two things to the world: our wounded selves and the announcement of the availability of a healing Jesus?

And what if a merciful God used the meager offering of our wounds and his availability as the way forward as the way of hope and healing for the world?

For many of us, we've realized that church as we once knew

it to be no longer exists in its same forms and expressions as we move into the future. What we can be sure of is that God's people are called to pay attention to and move toward pain and seize this ripe opportunity to join with Jesus in providing healing in His name. Right now is a time to heal.

The World Is Looking for Healers

In times of tragedy, a quote by the late, and still much revered, children's television personality Fred Rogers is often uttered: "When I was a boy and I would see scary things in the news, my mother would say to me, 'Look for the helpers. You will always find people who are helping.'"[16] We've all seen and experienced scary things – and we will continue to see and experience scary things. The helpers will always be present if we look for them. But because of what we've all been through, the world is looking for a specific kind of helpers: those who will help them heal. *People are looking for healers.*

Over the past several decades, Americans' spiritual needs have shifted significantly. Starting around the 1950s the collective pull from Americans was a search to know *how to truly be good.* A few decades later, it shifted primarily to a search to find *ultimate purpose and meaning*, followed by a collective search for *personal identity.* This led to another shift: a deep longing for *freedom.* Then the pandemic ushered in another seismic shift: *a collective longing for healing.*

But in order to join with God to help bring healing to a hurting world, we have to enter into a significant phase of *reorientation.* We must unlearn much of what we know. The late American futurist Alvin Toffler has been credited with saying, "The illiterate of the 21st century will not be those who cannot read or write. They will instead be those who cannot learn, unlearn, and relearn." To be the kinds of leaders the world will look to and identify as the healers, we must let go of the things we cherish deeply—our preferences, our models, our well-tested ways of thinking and being. Will we shrink back in fear or deny the depth of the changes required, or will we steel ourselves for the adventure of joining further with Jesus to bring healing to the world?

The Collective Need for Healing

We've all seen the pervasive nature of woundedness in our world. The time is ripe for the church to courageously move into the broken spaces and compassionately bind up the wounds of our local and global neighbors. The wounded are everywhere – and they are looking for the healers.

With a book about healing, there are, of course, countless questions about the subject at hand:
- How does healing actually work?
- Why is suffering so prevalent in the world – and what is its ultimate meaning?
- Why are those who are filled with deep faith not healed, while those with no faith at all experience healing?
- What is the role of science in healing, and is it compatible with faith?

As significant as these questions are, this book is not an attempt to answer them directly. My goal is to provide a hopeful guide, a framework for leading and serving in the new reality in an attempt to see the hope-filled, redemptive mission of God expand. Using the over-arching concept of death and resurrection in the Christian tradition, we'll explore how that arc becomes the path upon which we walk into the future. This death-and-resurrection approach is our Christian heritage, and it is our hopeful future.

The world is looking for the healers. *When they look, will they see us?*

Chapter 2

What Is the Hope We Have – and Have to Offer?

The main task of the minister is to prevent people from suffering for all the wrong reasons.[1]
—HENRI NOUWEN

He comforts us in all our troubles so that we can comfort others. When they are troubled, we will be able to give them the same comfort God has given us.
—2 CORINTHIANS 1:4 (NLT)

During Holy Week in 2019, fire ravaged Notre-Dame Cathedral in Paris. Built over 850 years ago, the famed cathedral engulfed with flames experienced a devastating loss in a matter of just a few hours. Crowds gathered in the streets and watched as it burned. While it will be rebuilt in due time, Parisians realized on that day the cathedral will never be the same again.

In December 2019, the novel COVID-19 coronavirus broke out in China. It spread quickly to every corner of the globe, affecting billions of people within just a few weeks. The damaging effects of the virus impacted America in the midst of Lent, the season of somber reflection where Christians reflect upon their mortality as we consider Jesus' own suffering and death. Millions of people around the world avoided crowds and stayed home. The U.S. Surgeon General predicted the death count from the virus would peak on Easter Sunday. We all realized what we once knew as normal would never be the same again.

Making Sense of Suffering

In the midst of loss, pain, and death, we are prone to ask significant questions: what is hope, and what does it look like? When I face loss, how can I experience hopeful sorrow instead of hopeless grief? Hope, of course, is always future-oriented. But we wonder in times of loss if there is any hope in the present, where it seems we are most in need of relief. These are significant questions—questions which cannot be answered sufficiently and completely here in this small book (or entirely this side of heaven). Yet, they are important questions; ones that should be voiced, and which are worthy of our time, energy, and attention.

Boston surgeon and renowned author Atul Gawande, a leading (and eloquent) voice in the medical profession, wrestled with this concept of suffering in his book *Being Mortal*: "I am in a profession that has succeeded because of its ability to fix. If your problem is fixable, we know just what to do. But if it's not? The fact that we have had no adequate answers to this question is trouble and has caused callousness, inhumanity, and extraordinary suffering."[2] What we long for is a hope-filled Christian theology of suffering that makes sense – or at least makes meaning. And so, if we explore the need for healing, then we must address suffering (albeit briefly) and how we are to make sense of it in the world.

Therefore, I want to offer a brief overview of a Christian approach to pain and suffering so as to orient our thinking, ground us in reality, and direct our gaze in the direction of our hope in Christ. This is no small task. A Christian understanding of suffering and loss starts with the stark acknowledgment that we all experience pain and loss, that no one can avoid suffering, and thus, people are too important in the eyes of God to try to be fixed. We fix cars and computers and dish washers, but not people. God does not always rescue us from suffering, despite His power to do so. The first element of a Christian understanding of suffering is to unabashedly acknowledge that *we cannot avoid suffering in our human condition.*

Suffering can be a wise teacher – if we can see it as such. As the author of Ecclesiastes wrote, "It is better to go to a house of mourning than to go to a house of feasting, for death is the destiny of everyone; the living should take this to heart… The heart of the wise is in the house of mourning, but the heart of fools is in the house of pleasure" (Eccl. 7:2,4). We ask ourselves the most pressing and significant questions of life more often when we gaze into a casket of a loved one than when we look at a couple on their wedding day. The Christian story teaches us that suffering can serve a greater purpose and deeper meaning beyond our immediate existence. Those who possess this faith-filled understanding often ask a different set of questions. Instead of *Why is this happening to me?* or *When will this suffering end?* they are asking *What is it God might be wanting to show me through this experience?* and *Where can my faith and hope deepen in my suffering?*

But we also learn *we are not alone in our suffering.* It is God who accompanies us. In suffering, we may wonder why God feels absent or why He is so silent. And yet, He *is* present, for He promises us such. The oft-repeated lines from the twenty-third Psalm remind us of this: "Even though I walk through the valley of the shadow of death, I will fear no evil for you are with me. Your rod and your staff, they comfort me" (v. 4). There is no promise God will send a cosmic helicopter to airlift us over Death Valley or that we will be rerouted with a divine GPS to another road to go around it entirely; instead, we are given the promise that as we travel life's journey, we will not be alone.

Additionally, suffering is most meaningful when others join us in it. Suffering is one of the most emotionally and mentally suffocating experiences in all of the human experience, and suffering alone can feel almost unbearable. Those who love us most dearly are those who compassionately walk with us in our times of pain; in doing so, they give us enough strength to simply put one foot in front of the other, even when we feel we can do no other. Like the faith of the friends of the paralytic in Mark 2, they attempted to do whatever was in their power to place their infirmed companion to the feet of Jesus. We learn in the story that Jesus has a propensity to heal those who are suffering, sometimes *because* of the presence of faith of compassionate helpers (Mk. 2:5).

The direct and indirect effects of pain and suffering we've all experienced have been staggering. Of course, we know the physical suffering from the virus. But it also has included additional realms. But suffering is most meaningful and bearable when it is embedded in knowing the suffering of Christ. Isaiah prophesied the coming of the Messiah and named him the suffering servant (Is. 52-53), the one who will come to save us, but who will suffer in the process. How comforting to know our rescuer is not aloof, out of touch, or unable to relate to our troublesome existence. He came to earth and experienced firsthand the same wounding experiences we have felt. And he still possesses scars on his hands and side to prove it.

A king who has suffered, a man who knew sorrow, a resurrected lamb who had been slaughtered – this Jesus is close at hand, knowing what we have been through, longing to befriend, rescue, redeem, set free, save, and ultimately heal. This is the Good News. As the hip hop artist, activist, and author Lecrae posited, "Wounds help us know we're not alone; scars help us know we can heal."[3] We all suffer. We can't avoid it. Suffering can hold a greater purpose and deeper meaning. It works to join meaning and hope together.

Look and Be Healed

In Numbers 21, we find a seemingly obscure yet disturbing story. The Israelites, having left Egypt, wandered in the wilderness for years with ever-increasing impatience with Moses, and with God. They complain, accuse, criticize, and even exaggerate the truth. God had taken care of them in the exodus from Egypt and even in their expedition through the wilderness – but now they'd had enough. And God had had enough, too. God released venomous snakes along the wilderness floor which bit the nation of Israel. Many became ill; others died – not for crimes of murder or rape or adultery, but because of their *complaining*. In the midst of their suffering, the people of God relented and repented.[4] Moses prayed, asking God to look down with kindness on His people. In an act of severe mercy, God told Moses to create a bronze snake and erect it on a wooden pole.[5] God told Moses to tell the people if they looked toward the snake affixed the pole they would be healed.[6]

Thousands of years later, under the cover of darkness, Jesus sat down with Nicodemus. The third chapter of John records the esteemed religious leader asking him questions about who he is and where he has come from. Jesus shared that He is the Messiah, the one the Jewish people had been waiting for all along.[7] Today, many people, even those with little or no religious background, recognize, and can even recite, John 3:16. And yet, few can recall the two verses prior: "Just as Moses lifted up the snake in the wilderness, so the Son of Man must be lifted up, that everyone who believes may have eternal life in him" (vv. 14-15).

Jesus disclosed to Nicodemus that the Messiah must become the cursed one who is hung on a wooden pole – and when people look to him, they will be healed. In doing so, he would take on our curse by hanging on a wooden cross and redeem the world. We experience sickness and death by the bite of sin; and we are healed and redeemed when we look to Jesus, who hung on a wooden pole. *The Good News of Jesus is a message focused squarely on healing.*

Have you ever looked closely at the blue decal on the side of an ambulance (often referred to as the worldwide emergency services' Star of Life), the label pin on a doctor's white coat, or the flag of the World Health Organization? It's a snake wrapped around a pole. This widely recognized symbol of medicine is often referred to as the Rod of Asclepius. Asclepius was the son of Apollo, the ancient god of healing mentioned in Homer's *The Iliad.*[8] According to ancient Greek mythology, he had five daughters, including Hygieia (the goddess of cleanliness) and Panacea (the goddess of universal remedy).[9] Dating back to the fifth century BC, the cult of Asclepius was significant and widespread; to date, archaeologists have found 732 healing temples and shrines (called *asclepieia*) throughout the Greek and Roman world in his honor.[10] Asclepius is often depicted holding a rod encircled by a serpent. His rod is often confused with the *caduceus,* the symbol of two snakes wrapped around a winged pole, which gained popularity in the twentieth century by way of the U.S. Armed Forces.[11] Many scholars believe the origin of the Rod of Asclepius and the *caduceus* can be traced back to the powerful stories found in Numbers 21 and John 3.[12] *Those who look to it will be healed.*

In the early phases of the pandemic, medical professionals—nurses, doctors, epidemiologists, and other medical technicians on the front lines—were hailed as heroes. These valiant men and woman risked much to serve those who had contracted the virus, even as medical facilities were overwhelmed, and supplies and equipment were in short supply. In cities all over the world, people went to their balconies and front porches at seven each evening to cheer, applaud, and bang pots and pans for these medical professionals coming on and off of their work shifts.

It was said not all heroes wear capes, some of them just wear masks. People were looking for – and lauding – the healers.

Sozo *Jesus*

If we could choose one word for the Church to embrace in this cultural moment, it would be the Greek word *sozo*. The word means to save, to deliver, and to rescue from danger or deliver from evil. But *sozo* has another meaning: to heal. Additionally, the Greek word *soteria* is translated as both salvation and healing. Our English word *salvation* finds its root in the Latin word *salve* – an ointment we put on our skin to soothe a burn, scrape, or blister. When we read a passage in the Gospels which records a person healed and we read another passage about someone who was saved, we're reading the same word.[13] Saving is healing, healing is saving. Even this idea of salvation, deliverance, and healing is bound together in the snake story in Numbers 21. God *saved* the people from slavery in Egypt, he *delivered* them from Pharaoh, and he *healed* them when they looked at the bronze snake. If this is God's nature, doesn't it make sense Jesus would offer all of that, too?

In the gospels, we see Jesus engaged in all sorts of *sozo* activities. The gospel of Luke, written from his unique perspective as a physician, is keenly attuned to the healing acts of Jesus. He highlighted Jesus' mission in the dramatic passage in Luke 4. Jesus had entered his hometown synagogue in Nazareth and stood to read the scroll of Isaiah.

Unrolling it, he found the place where it is written:

> *"The Spirit of the Lord is on me,*
> *because he has anointed me*
> *to proclaim good news to the poor.*
> *He has sent me to proclaim freedom for the prisoners*

> *and recovery of sight for the blind,*
> *to set the oppressed free,*
> *to proclaim the year of the Lord's favor."*
> *(vv. 18-21)*

Then he rolled up the scroll, gave it back to the attendant and sat down. The eyes of everyone in the synagogue were fastened on him. He began by saying to them, "Today this scripture is fulfilled in your hearing."

The mission of Jesus was rooted in the *sozo* reality: to speak good news to the poor, to free prisoners, to heal those who are sick.[14] At this, the people were amazed at what they heard. Yet within a few verses, and two brief references to Old Testament stories, they want to throw him off a cliff. What happened in the matter of a few sentences? Jesus stated his healing mission was not just for the Jews, God's chosen people; healing was available *for the whole world.* And the Jews were angry. They believed God cannot be available to everyone. He was only accessible to the chosen ones.

This concept of *sozo* is central to the mission of Jesus because it is rooted in the cosmic redemption plan of his Father to restore *shalom*. God's nature is embedded in healing. In the final chapter of the Old Testament God says, "Not a root or a branch will be left to them. But for you who revere my name, the sun of righteousness will rise with healings in its rays" (Mal. 4:1-2). Some translations say healing in its *wings.* Remember the woman suffering from her condition of bleeding? In many cases of healing found in the gospels, Jesus touched the infirmed. Sometimes he spoke a word and it happened. But in this instance, *the woman touched him*. She was ceremonially unclean; Jesus, a rabbi, who was ritually pure. Even in a crowd, touch was off-limits.

Yet, in her desperation, she reached out to touch the hem of his garment anyway. Why is this significant? Because in Jewish tradition, it was believed the edges of a garment or a prayer shawl were like wings. Could it have been that the woman was thinking of Malachi 4:2? Could it be that this woman believed Jesus was the one who *possessed healing in his wings*? Jesus stopped in his tracks and asked who had touched him. Peter believed the question was ludicrous amidst a crowd crushing in on him, but Jesus felt something change within him. Power had left his body. No wonder the woman trembled when she identified herself – the utter terror of being outed for contaminating a ceremonially clean rabbi. And yet, Jesus recognized her faith and acknowledged that, *yes, there is healing in my wings.* She had, indeed, been healed. In 1739, Charles Wesley penned the Christmas hymn *Hark! The Herald Angels Sing* highlighting Jesus' healing power:

> *"Hail the heaven-born Prince of Peace!*
>
> *Hail the Sun of Righteousness!*
>
> *Light and life to all He brings*
>
> *Risen with healing in His wings."*

The *salve* of Jesus.

The Shift from Saving to Healing

The Gospel message asserts that Jesus came to save, to deliver, to heal us from our sin-sick lives. We are in bondage in our sickness. When the Lord saves, he also heals; when he heals, he also saves. In Luke 9, Jesus gave his disciples (whom many scholars believe were teenagers) the ability to heal the sick, cast out demons, and proclaim the good news of the kingdom. Four out of the five times, Jesus commanded his disciples to declare the kingdom message; he also authorized them to heal the sick. [15] Jesus and his disciples were *bringers of healing* – and the healing opened up opportunities for preaching and teaching.[16] For Jesus' followers, healing involved paying attention to and joining with this *sozo* Jesus.

In our new reality, the gospel remains the same: Jesus' mission was a *sozo* mission. The billboards in America's heartland and the marquees of churches in every county across the country declare *Jesus Saves.* Yes, Jesus is our rescuer and all who look to him will be saved. Through him we find salvation. We can find true salvation in no other name (Acts 4:12). And while this is heart of the gospel's power, the *emphasis* and the entry point of our communication with the world must now be different. The spiritual-felt needs of people in the past allowed for the entry point of the good news to be *Jesus saves.* But now, with the spiritual- (and emotional-, physical-, mental-, relational-, and financial-) felt needs of our world, the most strategic entry point for communicating the Good News is *Jesus heals.* He is still *sozo* Jesus, but now this becomes the pressing need the world is looking to have met. It is still the same beautiful gem, but by turning the gem slightly, we see another shimmering facet of that beauty.

In John 5, Jesus arrives at the Pool of Bethesda and interacts with a lame man who longs to enter into the waters when stirred, but has no one to help him get in. He's stuck. Jesus looks at the man and asks directly, "Do you want to get well?" (Jn. 5:6). It is a question that penetrates us deeply in the midst of our collective woundedness. Jesus calls us to follow him – and in doing so, we become wounded healers in his name. We could label this call our *Sozo* Mandate. We must compassionately, humbly, and courageously ask, *"Do you want to get well?"*

The Paradox of Becoming a Wounded Healer

The late Catholic priest and author Henri Nouwen, in his prescient book *The Wounded Healer,* wrote,

> *The Messiah… is sitting among the poor, binding*
> *his wounds one at a time, waiting for the moment*
> *when he will be needed. So it is too with the minister.*
> *Since it is his task to make visible the first vestiges of*
> *liberation for others, he must bind his own wounds*
> *carefully in anticipation of the moment when he will*
> *be needed.*[17]

When followers of Jesus grasp this facet of the *sozo* gem they become healing communities. As Nouwen wrote, "not because wounds are cured and pains are alleviated, but because wounds and pains become the openings or occasions for new vision.… Community arises where the sharing of pain takes place, not as a stifling form of self-complaint, but as a recognition of God saving promises."[18]

If we are also wounded and in need of healing ourselves, how can we offer any hope and healing to the world? If we can't be the strong ones, how can we provide the healing which is so needed through our weakness? The great irony of the gospel is that we bring the news of healing when we ourselves need this good news, too. Henri Nouwen added: "We do not know where we will be two, ten, or twenty years from now. What we can know, however, is that man suffers and that the sharing of suffering can make us move forward."[19] He also wrote that the minister "is called to be the wounded healer, the one who must look after his own wounds but at the same time be prepared to heal the wounds of others."[20]

But as Dr. Susan Harper reminded me, we see in the gospels Jesus and the disciples healing others – *not themselves.* In our Western culture, which celebrates the Sovereign Self, we can be easily tempted to approach our suffering with the trendy self-help approach. The biblical vision, however, is not focused on self-help, nor is it giving us some seven-step formula for how I can heal myself. Instead, Jesus' vision is the opposite, rooted in the posture of self-sacrifice. Our calling, like John the Baptist, must involve employing our index fingers and pointing them outward toward Christ, the true Wounded Healer.

Kintsugi Gospel

Kintsugi is a Japanese art form dating back to the late fifteenth century. Kintsugi, which means "golden joinery," is an artistic expression of utilizing broken pottery by highlighting its flaws, rather than attempting to hide them. It is a similar approach to the Japanese art form called Wabi-Sabi, the art of finding beauty in imperfection.[21] When the broken shards are put back together again, gold powder is mixed into the adhesive in order to highlight the beauty of the brokenness. World renowned artist Mako Fujimura befriended a Kintsugi master, who leads workshops to help people experience the process of artistic repair and redemption.

Everyone brings a broken object to the workshop and the Kintsugi master shares with the participants that while they came to fix an object, they won't actually be fixing anything. Instead, they *will behold the brokenness and look at it long enough until they can see the beauty.* Then, and only then, will they try to mend it and try to make it new.[22] Kintsugi serves as a compelling metaphor for what it means to be a true healer in the name of Jesus. To approach this accurately, we must refrain from attempting to fix people. We must refuse to attempt to heal ourselves. We do not attempt to hide the brokenness. Instead, we attempt to see the fissures, to behold the brokenness, and invite Jesus, our Kintsugi master, to usher forth healing and wholeness. It is the gold adhesive of the good news of Jesus Christ which mends and brings beauty. It is a process with others of mending and trying to lead us toward something new (2 Cor. 5:17).

Jesus is our wounded healer who, in his outlandish grace, sent out his disciples with instructions to preach the good news, deliver those who are oppressed, and heal the sick (Mt. 10:7-8). And he sends us out as well to offer this hope to a world desperately in need of it. He longs for us to create Kintsugi art in a world filled with people with shards deeply embedded in their lives.

The world continues to look for healers. Will it count us among them? And if so, are we showing them Jesus, the wounded healer?

Chapter 3

How Did Jesus Heal — and How Are We to Join Him in the Healing Process?

The great illusion of leadership is to think that man can be led out of the desert by someone who has never been there.
—HENRI NOUWEN

*Praise the LORD, O my soul; all my inmost being, praise his holy name. Praise the LORD, O my soul, and forget not all his
benefits—who forgives all your sins and heals all your diseases.*
—PSALM 103:1-3

Perched atop the Corcovado mountain in the Tijuca Forest National Park, the famous Christ the Redeemer statue towers above Rio de Janeiro. Jesus looks down upon the city with his arms spread wide, offering himself to the world. On Easter night 2020, the city projected high-beam lights onto the statue depicting Jesus as a medical professional. Donning a white medical coat, a stethoscope around his neck, and the blue snake-encircled medical symbol on the left side of his coat, the word *OBRIGADO* shone across his legs – *thank you* in Portuguese.

The nation of Brazil expressed their gratitude for Jesus being our healer – and the world took notice.

Healing in the Gospels

Before we explore further how the world is looking for healers, we must first look to the wounded healer, Jesus. It may surprise you that there are more verses devoted to the healing ministry of Jesus in the gospels (physical, mental, emotional, and spiritual illnesses and raising people from the dead) than any other experience, including salvation.[1] Among all the activities of Jesus recorded in the four gospels, healing the sick and casting out demons were the most common.[2] Seventy-two times the four gospels mention Jesus healing or casting out demons.[3] He treated paralysis, immobility, skin diseases (such as leprosy), swelling (such as dropsy), blindness and muteness, fever, dysentery, a uterine hemorrhage and a withered hand to name a few.[4] He also healed others whose ailments aren't specifically mentioned (Mk. 7:31-37).

While Luke was the physician, it was Mark who recorded more instances of Jesus' healing work than any of the gospels. Almost a third of Mark is devoted to his miracles, including almost half of all the verses in the first ten chapters.[5] Mark highlights especially how Jesus brought forth healing through touch. His touch healed Peter's mother-in-law (Mk. 1:31) and brought a young girl back from the dead (5:41). He purposefully placed his hands on a leper, though it made him ceremonially unclean (and susceptible to contracting the disease). By caressing an older woman's hand, it caused her fever to leave. He healed by rubbing his hands on a blind man's eyes and sticking his fingers in a man's ears. When he touched a casket at a funeral procession, a young man was raised from the dead and offered back to his mother. At the same time, people wanted to touch Jesus. The sick pressed in on him, eager to touch him (3:10).[6]

And, as we saw earlier, in the story of the woman subject to bleeding, healing occurred when *others* touched him (Lk. 8:44).[7] Pediatric doctors, medical researchers, and neurobiologists have long reported on the importance of touch to our own physical, emotional, and relational development and wellbeing. The bonding between parents and newborns is nurtured with purposeful skin-to-skin contact. Conversely, evidence reveals the devastating consequences of stunted development and malformation when people, especially infants and toddlers, experience long periods of time without experiencing human touch.

When Jesus was willing to touch those inflicted by leprosy (known today as Hansen's disease), it was deeply significant. Leprosy turned the skin white and scaly; flesh would rot, and parts of the body would become deformed or fall off completely. In the ancient world, it was believed that breathing the same air of a leper was enough to contract the disease. The Mishnah outlined that contact with a leper or their possessions would make someone ceremonially unclean. Because of their hygienic and ceremonial impurities, lepers were required to keep their distance from others. The Pentateuch required lepers to look disheveled by wearing torn clothing and unkempt hair, cover their faces, and cry out, "Unclean! Unclean!" They were forced to live alone in leper colonies, oftentimes in the wilderness or an undesirable location outside of town.[8]

The Talmud specified a leper was forbidden to come within four cubits of another person – or one hundred cubits if an eastern wind was blowing. A cubit is approximately eighteen inches; thus, four cubits is approximately six feet of distance (sound familiar?). For an individual, a diagnosis of leprosy was a death sentence. Banished to a life of quarantine, social distancing, and isolation, Jesus' touch not only restored their physical state, but more significantly, it restored their emotional, relational, and communal standing as well. They were now freed from their

How Did Jesus Heal?

life-long sentence of isolation and reestablished their place back into a loving community. The healing of Jesus doesn't just take into account one aspect of a person's life; he desires healing for the whole person.

Healing permitted them to touch and be touched – literally and metaphorically – once again.[9] Jesus stated that curing leprosy was one of the physical signs he was the Messiah, the one Israel had been waiting for (Lk. 7:22). He even instructed his disciples to go and proclaim the message of the kingdom of God, as well as heal the sick, raise the dead, drive out demons, and cure those who have leprosy (Mt. 10:7-8). When everyone kept their distance from lepers, Jesus moved toward them, healing them, and reinstating their status within the community. *Obrigado.*

But Jesus also healed with his words. Sometimes the words were directed at sick people; other times they were uttered from afar, good news given to a messenger to send along to the infirm. Sometimes the healing occurred because of bold, tangible acts of faith in people's lives. Other times it occurred through prayer. (Isn't it interesting that in some instances even the Son of God needed to pray for healing to occur?)

And, most interesting of all, Jesus healed through *his spit.* On one occasion, Jesus spit on the ground, made mud with his saliva, and placed it on a blind man's eyes. On another occasion, he spit into his hands and then touched the tongue of a man unable to speak. And most shocking of all, outside of Bethsaida, he spit directly into a blind man's eyes and *then* put his hands on him.[10] In a COVID world, we are obsessed about hygiene. We are driven to wash hands multiple times a day, leaving many of us paranoid about sharing germs with others. To think about spitting in someone's face as an act of healing today seems unthinkable. Can we admit how surprising – and disgusting – this would have been if *we* were on the receiving end of one Jesus' mucus miracles? But maybe that's exactly the point: healing isn't always nice and pretty. It's messy and earthy, and, at times, even nasty. But freedom, restoration, and healing are still the end results.

Jesus' healing was motivated out of both a deep compassion for those who were sick, as well as an evident disdain for evil and destructive forces. The text often records Jesus rebuked the demons, speaking harshly to them.[11] What motivated his healing was this: *Jesus longed for people to be free and whole.* Healing, at its foundational level, is about spiritual, emotional, relational, physical, and psychological freedom and wholeness. The *sozo* Jesus at work.

Offering Our Wounds to Others

Isn't it both deeply hopeful and utterly astounding that Jesus' post-resurrection body still bore visible, physical scars? Thomas, so adamant in his doubt of Jesus' resurrection, when the other disciples told him Jesus had risen from the dead, offered this response: "Unless I see the nail marks in his hands and put my finger where the nails were, and put my hand into his side, I will not believe" (Jn. 20:25). What a gruesome, graphic, and crass response to utter about your dead rabbi! When Jesus appeared to his disciples several days after his resurrection, Jesus focused his attention, not on the believers in the room, but on the doubter. Jesus invited Thomas, the one who had just uttered a grotesquely inappropriate in-your-face response of disbelief, to touch his wounds, the wounds that brought healing to the world. "Put your finger here; see my hands. Reach out your hand and put it into my side" (Jn. 20:27). Jesus met Thomas in his doubt and invited him to not only see his wounds; he wanted him to touch them, too. Jesus knew that this experience would lead to Thomas' own healing.

Four hundred years ago, the Italian painter Caravaggio depicted this dramatic scene in his famous piece of art *The Incredulity of Saint Thomas.* In the piece, Jesus has his cloak open, revealing his chest and side. He carefully and purposefully takes Thomas' hand and guides his finger into his wounded side. Thomas' brow is furrowed with focus and astonishment, while two other disciples look over his shoulder in hushed amazement. Jesus vulnerably, compassionately, and patiently offers himself to the doubter. If we are to follow Jesus, our wounded healer, then we must do the same.

Joining the Wounded Healer

But how do we join God's mission by following the example of Jesus in a posture of healing for the sake of a hurting world? This death-to-resurrection leadership journey is ironic: in the desire to lead others to healing, we will find that we ourselves are often healed the most. And we may experience elements of death more than others—and that death, literal or metaphorical, may even include us. As we seek to follow the resurrected, scar-bearing Christ, we must name several realities.[12]

1. We must healthily embrace our own failure.

Jesus' scars, as with most scars, were a constant and tangible reminder of what should not have been. And they remained after the resurrection. That chronological detail matters. Our bodies may not carry the physical evidence of scars, but every one of us bears scars on our souls, our minds, our hearts. Why? Because we are humans, yes. But even more so, because we seek to care for people. The great irony of Christian service is we are called to bear the pain of others who wound us while simultaneously teaching people to experience healing from Jesus. He invites, empowers, and unleashes us to offer healing to the world. *Can we really truly lead well if we have not been deeply wounded first?* Without experiencing failure, disappointment, loss, and pain how can we empathize with and lead others who have experienced – and are experiencing –these things? Without these experiences, we could easily become arrogant, distant, unmerciful, and prone to condescending legalism in its most lethal form.

Failure has a way of teaching us things success never can. Failure is what gives us our credibility, our authority, to lead as wounded healers who follow the Wounded Healer. Our open wounds open doors to embrace grace-filled opportunities of true healing. We learn to embrace failure—not in a nihilistic manner, but in knowing failure is most often the fertile soil of our own growth and maturity, though it hurts like hell. It is not a matter of *will I fail?* but instead *how will I respond when I experience it?* Will we face our failures and seek to learn from them, or will we do all we can to deny, ignore, or curse its existence?

2. We must reveal our wounds to others.

Once we've done the difficult, vulnerable inner work of naming and acknowledging, then – and only then – are we able to begin to reveal our wounds to others. This is deeply disorienting – and yet also extremely clarifying and liberating. We must appropriately model for others, those inside and outside of the church, that we are *humans first.* The world is not repulsed by this. They know we are human, but they wonder why we don't often act like one. Interestingly, the world is deeply attracted to authentic, courageous, humble, and vulnerable brokenness. When we model for others what courageous, authentic, humble weakness looks like, it builds deeper connection, trust, and empathy with others.

The long-held expectation that we must always be the strong ones is rapidly changing. People are desiring, more than ever before, for people – especially followers of Jesus – who can laugh and cry in the same conversation, who can admit their faults and sins long before someone else catches them in it. They can speak of their own woundedness with tears in their eyes and hope on their lips. This is the kind of person the world looks to—the kind who is stumbling in the direction of healing alongside of others. When we do this, we are inviting others on the journey toward healing, too.

3. We must grieve the loss of certainty we once knew.
In times of loss and grief, it can be tempting to put our head down, try to move forward as quickly as possible, and attempt to get back to business. But if we are not careful, doing so can actually add to the pain and grief. Our world has just gone through upheaval. Those we know and love have gone through upheaval. We have gone through our own upheaval. We once felt certain about the way the world worked, confident in our approaches to ministry, settled in our understanding of the future; now, all this has been thrown off course. Some of these significant changes were necessary and good; others are difficult to let go of.

For the most part, we liked the old reality better. We knew our place. We were accepted, received as an expert in the field as we drew from our years of education or experience or reputation. Now we are required to learn new sets of skills, think in new ways, and approach the world with more courage, trust, openness, and vulnerability than ever before. And we need to grieve this. It's a significant loss. Many people keep a daily gratitude list. Maybe in heavy seasons we help people develop grief lists. Naming things has a way of taming things. Our grief should not be ignored. Naming our own areas of grief helps us to locate the pain and remember our own scars we carry on our hands and side.

4. We must acknowledge and repent of our idols – many which are rooted in Christendom.
What many of us grieve about the loss of certainty is often tied directly to our understanding of church within the Christendom model. We liked it when we could assume people came to church on the weekend to hear us preach – and in person. We

grew to enjoy it when people gave to the church without much prodding or convincing. We were pleased by the benefits of sitting in our study and reverently preparing for the weekend's sermon for hours on end. We enjoyed the benefits of the Church and her leaders being well respected. But these can no longer be assumed true.

Worse yet, some of us have come to love these benefits and advantages more than Christ and his Church. The excruciating part of all of this grief is knowing much of it is rooted in our own idolatry. We're constrained by decisions that must be made in order to maintain lifestyles – of others and ourselves – that we don't want to surrender. Ironically, this kind of courageous vulnerability may expose us to more pain and woundedness.

Yet here is the good news: the Church in North America is not in decline. The Western Christendom forms of church are certainly in decline. There is no denying this. But let me be clear: I'm not convinced the true Church of Jesus Christ is. Yes, moving forward into a new reality will, in all likelihood, mean presiding in some capacity over the funeral of Christendom. And yet, doing so will usher in the opportunity to experience the resurrected existence of Jesus' true church emerging out of the grave in new and powerful ways. Christendom dies, but what might God be resurrecting? In this process, we become the kinds of people who offer healing because we all have experienced death and resurrection first.

Look Around

The beginning of the Gospel of John records John the Baptist announcing the coming of Jesus. When people thought John was the redemptive solution for the whole world, he quickly refuted it; instead, he pointed in Jesus' direction and said it's not me, it's *him.* He even told his own disciples to leave him and start following Jesus instead.

But later in Jesus' ministry, John was thrown in prison. He had his doubts about Jesus. Had he gotten it wrong? Was there someone else who was to fulfill the hopes of the nation? To settle the matter from prison, he sent his own followers to Jesus to ask the bold and direct question: "Are you the one who is to come, or should we expect someone else?" (Lk. 7:18). The text states Jesus had just healed a wide variety of people with various illnesses, ailments, and sicknesses. Jesus had every right to respond angrily, a drop-the-mic zinger laced with holy indignation and acute sarcasm inflicting deep shame. He could have been offended or felt betrayed. Wagging his finger and raising his voice, Jesus had every reason to retort, "Who else do you think I am, John? Don't you remember: *you're* the one who prepared the way for my arrival? *You're* the who baptized *me,* for crying out loud!" Instead, he doesn't offer a lengthy list of doctrinal points or systematized theological distinctives about his nature. Instead, he told John's disciples to look around. Pay attention. Notice. See how people have been impacted by what he had done – and is doing.

The blind now see.

The crippled now walk.

Those who had leprosy are cured.

The deaf have the ability to hear.

There were people walking around who used to be dead.

The poor hear good news speaking directly to their condition.

Jesus, in all likelihood, was alluding to Isaiah 35, a chapter written to a group of deflated, confused, and doubting people, wondering if God had forgotten, neglected, and abandoned them. Isaiah states the way God would save his people would be through healing.

Strengthen the feeble hands,
　　steady the knees that give way;
say to those with fearful hearts,
　　"Be strong, do not fear;
your God will come,
　　he will come with vengeance;
with divine retribution
　　he will come to save you."

Then will the eyes of the blind be opened
　　and the ears of the deaf unstopped.
Then will the lame leap like a deer,
　　and the mute tongue shout for joy.
(vv. 3-6a, NIV)

Jesus' response shows he is doing *exactly* what God said would be done through his saving work for the world: healing people. Do you see it? As British missiologist Christopher Wright pointed out, the importance of the word *then*, repeated in the end of this passage. "When? When would such things happen? When 'your God will come.' So if these things were clearly happening around Jesus, then the big question was: Who had come? Who was Jesus?"[13]

The way Jesus identified himself, the way he offered evidence he was the Messiah, was through his healing. He mentioned his healing ministry *first*, and then about his preaching of the Good News. Jesus' response was stark and direct: *look for the healing.*

And when we catch a glimpse of this healing Jesus and experience it ourselves, our response can be *obrigado.*

Chapter 4

How Will the Church Be the Body of Christ to a Hurting World?

Molested, abused, abandoned, arrested, accused, and stranded
I grew up with all this trauma, it's nothing, forget it happened
Ten years later it show up, life is starting to blow up.
   —LECRAE, "RESTORE ME"

For I was hungry and you gave me something to eat, I was thirsty and you gave me something to drink, I was a stranger and you invited me in, I needed clothes and you clothed me, I was sick and you looked after me, I was in prison and you came to visit me.
   —MATTHEW 25:35-36

On November 13, 2015, a series of carefully coordinated terrorist attacks by ISIL rattled Paris. People around the world flooded social media with messages of condolences saying: "Our thoughts and prayers are with Paris." Comedian Anthony Jeselnik, in his standup routine the night of the attacks, boldly stated why he would dare to make fun of people who had offered up heartfelt "thoughts and prayers" on the day of an international tragedy: "Do you know what [thoughts and prayers] are worth? *Nothing.* Less than nothing. You are not giving your time, your money, or your compassion. All you are doing is saying, 'Don't forget about me today.'"[1] While the audience responded with nervous laughter, Jeselnik was making no attempt to be funny. And Jeselnik was not alone. Many Parisians responded the same way: *we don't want your thoughts and prayers. We want your help.* Paris was looking for healers. Today, there are more than just Parisians looking for healing. Do we see them?

Certainly, for those committed to the Way of Jesus, thoughts and prayers are a wonderful and expected response to a horrible tragedy – or any time for that matter. But what Paris was asserting was they'd gladly receive those heart-felt prayers if people put legs to them. Christian activist and author Shane Claiborne shared, "When people say, 'All we can do is pray,' that's not true. There are all kinds of things that we need to do to supplement our prayers and put feet on them… One of the greatest mysteries of our faith is that God actually invites us to be a part of the miracle of changing and healing and redeeming the world."[2] Actionless prayers can often create more pain. As we've experienced a collective global PTSD, many are saying the same thing. *We need help.* We should pray, yes – but the Church is called to more than just prayer. While medical professionals are trained to be first responders, the church is called to be spiritual and emotional first responders.

A Brief Summary of Global Pain and Christian Compassion

During the pandemic, the word *unprecedented* was used an unprecedented number of times. It may be a new phenomenon to us in our generation, but they have been the norm for centuries.[3]

- During the Peloponnesian War, the Plague of Athens killed an estimated 75,000-100,000 people.

- The Plague of Justinian (most commonly known as the bubonic plague) brought about an estimated thirty to fifty million deaths.[4]
- The Black Death spread across Europe, Asia, and into parts of Africa in the fourteenth century wiping out approximately *one-third of all the people in the world.*
- From the beginning of the fifteenth century through the middle of the seventeenth century, Europe experienced a significant outbreak of the plague on average *every nine years.*[5]
- Smallpox spread globally and lasted more than three hundred years, wiping out an estimated fifty-six million people.
- Cholera created *seven* pandemics over a span of 150 years, eliminating an estimated one million people.
- Yellow fever killed 150,000 people; scarlet fever killed tens of thousands more.[6]
- The Spanish flu began in Europe and the United States and saw four waves of the disease from 1918 through 1920, killing an estimated forty to fifty million people worldwide.[7]

Needless to say, plagues and epidemics have been around for quite some time.

In the midst of such atrocities, persecution, and tragedy, including plagues and epidemics, Christians were known as compassionate first responders. Followers of Jesus cared for the sick, despite immense risk and danger to their own wellbeing. Motivated by the bone-deep conviction of the *imago dei*, they believed every human was specially created in the image of God. I'm inspired by these early Christians who were seen favorably, not because they cared for their own sick, but because they also cared for those outside the Christian community, *including those who were persecuting them.*

St. Ignatius, reflecting upon Jesus' words that it was the sick who needed a doctor, not the healthy (Mk. 2:17), used the term *Christus medicus* (Christ the Physician).[8] Since at least the fourth century, pastors have been known as spiritual physicians.[9] Eusebius, bishop of Caesarea and a prominent church historian, recorded that the region had been deeply impacted by war, famine *and* a ravaging plague at the same time around AD 312. The response of the Christians was so compassionate that Eusebius recorded "their deeds were on everyone's lips, and [the pagans] glorified the God of the Christians."[10] Imagine if that's how a doubting, hurting world responded to our response today?

In the late fourth century, hospitals were first created through the efforts of Basil the Great in Caesarea and John Chrysostom in Constantinople.[11] Later, the medieval church established hospices.[12] How could a little religious sect around AD 30 grow to a world-wide following of millions of adherents within just a few centuries? Sociologist Rodney Stark, in his book *The Rise of Christianity*, sought to answer the question. One of the main reasons he found was that when everyone else ran and hid, Christians remained to care for the sick:

> *Christianity revitalized life in Greco-Roman cities by providing new norms and new kinds of social relationships able to cope with many urgent urban problems. To cities filled with the homeless and the impoverished, Christianity offered charity as well as hope. To cities filled with newcomers and strangers, Christianity offered an immediate basis for attachments. To cities filled with orphans and widows, Christianity provided a new and expanded sense of family. To cities torn by violent ethnic strife, Christianity offered a new basis for social solidarity. And to*

> *cities faced with epidemics, fires, and earthquakes,*
> *Christianity offered effective nursing services.*[13]

Their willingness to serve and suffer on the front lines and extend radical hospitality in the midst of great need was *their most effective form of evangelism.*

I'm deeply inspired when I read about Cyprian. In AD 250, a plague spread from northern Africa to Europe and swept through Carthage in North Africa. The bishop, Cyprian, encouraged Christians in the city to donate their resources to care for the sick. He urged the rich to donate funds and the poor to volunteer their time. The Church organized programs in several cities for systematic health care – all while Christians were experiencing massive persecution. Their love was so radical, people couldn't help but notice their love.

The emperor Decius ordered clergy to be arrested. Sacrifices offered to pagan gods were mandated; those who refused were put to death. In spite of all of this, Christians extended compassion not just to other Christians, but also to the pagans – the ones who were attempting to kill them for their faith. This is known as the Plague of Cyprian. Cyprian was not to blame for spreading the plague. No, just the opposite. He was known for spreading radical compassion during the plague. His organizing efforts led to care and healing – and it led the world to remember the plague by his name. The world couldn't help but take notice and embrace these Christians with open arms.[14] Early Christians believed epidemics and plagues were too significant for God to waste – so they joined him in the healing. Don't stories like this make you stick our chest out with healthy pride knowing we stand on the shoulders of faith-filled people like these?

About this time, another devastating plague ripped through Alexandria, claiming half of the city's population. Dionysius, the bishop of the city, wrote to leaders to oversee the care of the sick, even at the risk of losing their own lives. He recounted the pagans "pushed away those with the first signs of the disease and fled from their dearest. They even threw them half dead into the roads and treated unburied corpses like refuse in hopes of avoiding the plague of death." While the pagans ran for the hills, the Christians ran to the sick, the hurting, and the dying.[15]

Then, five hundred years ago, the plagues swept through Europe. Students and faculty of Wittenberg where Martin Luther taught were told to evacuate the city. Luther, however, stayed and continued to teach, preach, and care for the sick. Johann Hess, a pastor in Breslau, Germany, wrote Martin Luther and asked him if Christians were obligated to stay and help or if they were free to head to the country where the masses had evacuated. Luther penned a response titled, "Whether One May Flee From A Deadly Plague." His response was both theological and practical:

Therefore, I shall ask God mercifully to protect us. Then I shall fumigate, help purify the air, administer medicine, and take it. I shall avoid places and persons where my presence is not needed in order not to become contaminated and thus per chance in fact and pollute others, and so caused their death as a result of my negligence.[16]

Luther also encouraged Hess and others to prepare themselves so they might be ready for death, should it arrive at their doorstep. But essentially Luther's advice can be boiled down to one main thought: unless one was a public servant (a doctor or nurse, a public official, a minister, a master of servants, etc.) fleeing the city was permitted, as long as one wasn't abandoning, neglecting, or "depriving their neighbors of anything, but first meeting their obligations toward them."[17]

About 150 years ago, on the small island of Molokai in the archipelago of Hawaii, a large colony of lepers was established, a location the healthy dared not visit for fear of contracting the disease. A healthy, thirty-three-year-old Catholic priest and missionary from Belgium, Father Damien de Veuster, arrived via boat with a life-long call from God to serve the lepers. On May 4, 1873, the bishop of Honolulu, Father Maigret, joined Father Damien on the journey and offered him one final opportunity to change his mind. Father Damien declined. With steeled resolve he stated, "I am ready to be buried alive with those poor wretches." Able-bodied, he joined the colony, loved his new community, built homes and developed infrastructure, served those who were ill and isolated, and shared the message of Jesus. Twelve years after he arrived on the island, he discovered his feet had become leprous. Four years later, he died of the disease and was laid to rest in the leper's cemetery he helped build. The Catholic Church later canonized him into sainthood.[18] Father Damien ran toward the pain until he could no longer feel it.[19]

It's clear Christianity offered significant contributions to healthcare, providing a foundation for the whole tradition of Western medical care ministries.[20] Catholics have long excelled in organizing medical charities, most notably hospitals. In the nineteenth century, Florence Nightingale took what she learned in her service as a deaconess and traveled to England where she founded a school of nursing. Clara Barton founded the Red Cross in order to address epidemics such as yellow fever and cholera. William and Catherine Booth started The Salvation Army to help those who were suffering under poverty, addiction, loneliness, and despair while serving those in need of physical, emotional, mental, and spiritual healing. Even today, countless Christians serve through long-term and short-term mission trips, many of them in some form of medical missions. There are numerous ministries and organizations who have served for decades among poor and hurting populations. The Christian story is full of faith-filled, compassionate sisters and brothers who rolled up their sleeves and moved toward the hurting, the sick, the wounded, and the dying, even when others turned and ran.

The Church as a Field Hospital

The irony of the gospel message is that our power is found in our weakness, not our strength. But how can weakness possess any power? Is this not a glaring oxymoronic statement? Paul heard these words directly from Jesus: "My grace is sufficient for you, for my power is made perfect in weakness." Paul then stated boldly, "Therefore, I will boast all the more gladly about my weaknesses, so that Christ's power may rest on me" (2 Cor. 12:9). In the economy of the kingdom, weakness is our uniqueness.

Earlier, I recounted the fire that destroyed the Notre-Dame Cathedral. Over its 850-year history, it served as a place of refuge, relief, and healing. During the diseases and plagues in the Middle Ages, it served, quite literally, as a hospital, caring for six hundred patients at a time. It was also known as a place connected with healing miracles, often credited to St. Genevieve, the patron saint of Paris, who was venerated as a healer. A statue of her was placed on the cathedral's façade, prominently displayed above the entrance, along with a series of stained-glass windows depicting her life. Many of St. Genevieve's relics were stored in the spire and were destroyed in the fire, but her example and commitment to healing lives on.[21] The Church needs more people like St. Genevieve.

As the common adage goes, the church is not to be a museum for saints, but a hospital for sinners. In a world of pain and woundedness, the Church possesses a diagnostic role by identifying the signs of the times, a preventive role by creating an "immune system" in a society in which the malignant viruses of fear, hatred, violence, and nationalism are prevalent, and a role of rehabilitation by overcoming the traumas of the past through forgiveness.[22]

Where Should We Look?

A Christian response of love in the midst of a global tragedy is far from unprecedented. We're grateful to read stories of the past, but what about the future? Our call is to train our eyes – and help other people look for those in need of healing, even when it isn't always apparent. If the world is ever going to consider looking in the direction of church for its healing, we must first look in these ten specific areas.

1. See the Bible as a book written to traumatized people.
Consider who the Bible was most frequently written to. The Scriptures – both Old and New Testaments – were not written to comfortable, healthy people in power, but instead to a group of discouraged, displaced, distressed, and oppressed people marked by trauma. Think of the stories of traumatized people found in the Bible:
- The runaway and abused slave girl Hagar.
- Joseph was sold into slavery *by his own brothers.*
- Noah's family witnessed the destruction of the world through a global flood.
- Jonah was trapped in the stomach of a large fish for a few days after suffering a life-threatening squall.
- The entire nation of Israel was enslaved and in exile by the oppressive, unjust pagan nation of Egypt.
- Moses was on the run for his life after murdering an Egyptian.
- The prophet Elijah fled because of the death threat from evil tyrants.

- Job's immense emotional, relational, and physical suffering.
- Tormented parents in Bethlehem who had experienced infanticide. Mary would have been friends and neighbors with mothers whose baby boys had been murdered by King Herod.
- Mary and Joseph fled to Egypt as refugees.
- Mary Magdalene was delivered from not one, but *seven* demons (and later became one of Jesus' closest followers).
- John the Baptist experienced a gruesome beheading at a royal banquet.
- Jesus suffered naked on the cross through harrowing crucifixion.
- Early Christians were arrested, persecuted, and executed in the book of Acts.

In the pages of our Bible, trauma is *everywhere*. It is essential we read Scripture through the lens of trauma. The book of Lamentations and much of the Psalms contain raw and desperate prayers of suffering people. If the Old Testament was written mostly to the people of God who were in exile, and if both testaments were written to people who were oppressed, traumatized, and suffering, how might this shape how we read our Bibles today?[23]

One of the simplest and most practical ways for congregations to cultivate a good kingdom imagination as healers is to allow the biblical text to shape our individual and collective thinking. If we can see the overarching story of Scripture – the shalom-creating God and a shalom-rejecting humanity, who are traumatized and in need of being saved, delivered, and healed by a shalom-bringing Jesus – our people will begin to see more fully the vision of what it means to live like Jesus. But it may mean pastors need to preach other difficult texts not often preached on, such as the Psalms of Lament.

You may want to start by journeying through the gospel of Mark, which, as we explored earlier, is laden with healings, right from chapter one. Or, you may want to study and explore Dr. Luke's gospel and pay close attention to those stories of healing. Look at the parables about healing and trauma. Consider the story of the Good Samaritan in Luke 10. The Samaritan soothed the wounded man with oil and wine and bandaged his wounds. He then took him to an inn to care for him further. He even handed the innkeeper two silver coins and told *him* to be a part of the healing process, too. Have you ever pondered this story through the lens of healing?

As you immerse yourself in the stories of healings in the gospels, pause and read them slowly. Ask and discuss with others where there are wounds and brokenness and where we long to experience healing in our own lives. And then ask where we might join God in his work of healing in specific and practical ways. Inquire where there are areas, groups of people, or individuals in our community who are hurting and in need of experiencing radical compassion. Where can we be the *sozo* people of God?

2. Listen to – and tell – stories.

Stories have healing power because stories connect us. If trauma and woundedness is the experience of disconnection, conversely then, healing is about connection. When people tell their stories, and they know their stories are being heard by someone who cares about them, it often allows healing to blossom. Artists, musicians, poets – even comedians – share that the basis of their craft is rooted in the ability to experience healing through the expression of their reality. This often leads to others being healed in the process, too, because the act of storytelling itself offers healing. In addition to hearing people's stories, we can also tell the stories of others. We can start to tell the stories of everyday, ordinary heroes who are faithfully following Jesus by being bringers of healing and bearing their own wounds. Catch people doing things *right.* Telling inspiring stories of healers inspires more stories of healers. Challenge people to follow the plethora of *sozo* opportunities which exist around the world — and across the street. By giving them a framework by which they can see Jesus and the world, it will help your people realize the invitation and command to follow Jesus into the world. We cannot expect people to be mobilized into mission if there is no vision for which they can look to and if they are not instructed, equipped, and taught how to do it themselves.

3. *Look for the trauma.*

We can't help people heal if we aren't aware of their trauma, and it doesn't help that the word trauma is a bit slippery. It can feel vague. We can say to our friend that watching our team lose in the championship was traumatic, or we may have swerved out of the way of an oncoming car and narrowly avoided a head-on collision which left us shaking for the next thirty minutes. Or, we experience trauma which remains with us decades after a horrific incident occurs. But a true understanding of trauma is seen as the inability to process our grief or resolve our pain. It can be any life event that leads to feeling alone and without help or support.[24] It affects your entire being – mind, body, and spirit. As Bessel van der Kolk wrote, "Trauma is something that overwhelms your coping capacities and confronts you with the thought: 'Oh my God, it's all over, and there's nothing I can do. I'm done for. I may as well die.'"[25]

One of the most practical places to start is by growing in awareness. Consider conducting a trauma audit in your church, among your circle of friends or within your neighborhood. Simply list out the people who've experienced trauma and the type of trauma they've experienced. What are the themes or specific types of trauma present in your context? What might be the root of it? How are you noticing the people you've listed being kept from flourishing because of their trauma?[26]

By being aware of the issues right in front of you, it can help to shape your prayers and give you a softer heart, more perceptive eyes, and more awareness which can allow you to look for ways to care and assist others through the healing process. Their trauma may require professional help beyond your level of expertise or education, but you may be able to play a key role in introducing them to individuals or important resources. Suffering people need empathy and acceptance – to be met where they are. We wait. We don't speak. We don't explain or rationalize. We are simply present. We listen as ones who bear witness. We lament with people in their Psalm 88 moment. All so they can know and experience God's presence in their pain.[27]

4. Explore your own wounds and trauma.
If we are to be healers, we need to address our own trauma and woundedness. God, in his undeserved kindness, uses people to help in the healing process who are also in their own process of healing as well.[28] We must position ourselves in ways where God can do his healing work in us, even as he provides his healing work through us. We must be aware that trauma brings a whole assortment of issues to our minds, bodies, and souls: shame, exposure, confusion, fear, loss of joy, feelings of powerlessness, isolation, depression, insomnia, loss of trust, loss of pleasure, distortion of reality, anger, a desire to escape, anxiety, and hyperawareness, among other things.

As caregivers and healers, we must make sure we are receiving care and healing ourselves. Richard Rohr wrote, if we do not transform our pain, we will most assuredly transmit it – usually to those closest to us. Therefore, we must do the difficult inner work of processing with ourselves, with God, and with other trusted, wise, and safe individuals.

One of my favorite questions, which I ask myself and other leaders and caregivers, is: *What do you do when you are BLASTED?* The word BLASTED is an acronym, which stands for Bored, Lonely, Angry/Anxious/Afraid, Stressed, Tired, Envious, and Discouraged/Depressed. We have our own default settings for how we cope in these situations. Some of our responses are healthy, some quite unhealthy. But if we can name them, we can begin to see behind the curtain of our soul and of our faith. Naming things has a way of taming things; and ultimately, naming things has a way of changing things. If they are healthy responses, we should continue to press into them. If they are unhealthy, we are to look for ways to replace them with healthy responses.

Drilling down a bit deeper, we must look for ways to slowly and carefully process our own trauma. Here are questions you could use for personal reflection:

- When was the last time I shared the deep pains of my heart with someone other than my immediate family?
- How can I – or do I – bring these pains before God?
- What is my greatest source of chronic stress?
- What are the signs I am not coping well?
- What routine activities could I engage in to help manage stress?
- What routine activities should I stop doing?
- What beliefs do I hold about my current stress or woundedness that need evaluation?
- Who can join with me in order to help in my own pain?
- Where do I need to put boundaries?
- What hinders me from good self-care as I seek to care for others?[29]

5. Look for tears – in others and in yourself.
Frederick Buechner famously wrote:

> *Whenever you find tears in your eyes, especially unexpected tears, it is well to pay the closest attention. They are not only telling you something about the secret of who you are, but more often than not God is speaking to you through them of the mystery of where you have come from and is summoning you to where, if your soul is to be saved, you should go to next.*[30]

But this is not just true for us; we must peer into the eyes of others who shed tears. The fact that liquid leaks out of our faces is a gracious gift from God. When we are overwhelmed or scared or scarred or saddened or beyond grateful, our physical bodies realize it is too much to handle on its own; it must be released. These are sacred moments. Theology is built into our biology. I'm grateful God designed us to release tears, not out of our big toe or our left elbow, but out of our face, the most significant relational receptor on the human body. When we cry, our bodies send others an important message: *pay attention to me. Something sacred is happening right now. I need people to see me in this moment.* When tears are present, we should not be afraid or apologetic. This is an important moment.

I'm reminded in these sacred moments: tears are liquid prayers. When I sit with people who begin to cry, I seek to hold space for God's presence to be felt. When appropriate, I gently remind people that tears are liquid prayers. I often ask if they are able to articulate the words their face is praying in the moment. These are some of the most truth-filled moments of life.

6. Look for everyday practices and elements where healing can occur.

If we're not careful, we can assume healing can only happen in a doctor's examination room, on a counselor's couch, or when a professional is writing a prescription. Certainly, those spaces are significant and important. But people heal in a myriad of other ways – ways which are less formal, more relational, and available to participate in any given day.

Healing happens when people strongly sense they are in a safe place to tell their story – and to hear others tell their stories. The most impactful stories are ones of courageous vulnerability where others want to whisper, "Me, too." Like Jesus, physical touch and embrace – when wise and appropriate – are other ways in which people heal. Being present with others and showing up. Laughing together. Crying together. Telling stories together. Reflecting and processing safely with others. Praying together. Sitting in silence and stillness with no expectation. These are practices, activities, and spaces available to each and every one of us. You don't need a degree or loads of experience to engage in their practices with others who are wounded.

We must possess the mindset that we are *called to be people of blessing*. Yes, it can be messy, painful, uncomfortable, and awkward – it comes with the territory. But when the everyday people of God bless others in the name of Jesus, those opportunities are ripe for healing. Do we see these ordinary opportunities possessing power for healing to occur in people's lives? If so, all that it requires is to just show up. There is power in presence.

7. *Look for the healers who are already in your midst.*

In every congregation, there are people who spend their vocational lives helping others heal. Maybe your church is comprised of several doctors, nurses, physical therapists, dentists, trainers, and/or other medical professionals. Maybe you're one of them. What would it look like if your church offered free medical services at your facility for those who don't have health insurance? How might you invite medical professionals to come together and brainstorm, pray, and collaborate on how they might combine their unique callings together to serve in the name of Jesus? How might they pray for their patients and clients, as well as for one another, that God would use them in order to respond to physical suffering with compassionate presence and a tangible hope to bring shalom through the power of the Spirit? How might we link arms in order to kick up some good kingdom mischief?

Many medical professionals do more than provide programmatic medical healing services. They also sit and listen gently to patients who are anxious about their medical issues. They patiently help others navigate insurance and prescription drug options so they can afford their health care. They look their patients in the eyes, pray with them before leaving the room, and encourage those who need spiritual support to connect with their churches. All of these simple acts of care help to offer healing as a medical care professional – and they need to be celebrated.

And, in all likelihood, your church also includes counselors, therapists, social workers, school counselors, psychiatrists, mental health support specialists, and others who spend their weeks helping in the mental and emotional health fields. What would it look like for these women and men to dream together how they might provide mental and emotional healing in the community? What if they felt empowered, unleashed, and released – with full support and encouragement from their pastor – to serve in Jesus' name? What if counseling services could be subsidized or fully covered through local churches in order for those who desperately need them?

What if the businesspeople in your church – those in the financial industry, small business owners, bank employees, and accountants – worked together to provide financial counseling services to those in need? What if they bound together to provide debt relief classes for the community or offered to help the unemployed brush up their resumes or strengthen their job interview skills?

What if the artists in your community rallied together to provide sacred space to help people articulate the inner groaning in ways words simply cannot? What if they provided art therapy for children and adults free of charge for those in your church and broader community? Or what if writers created poems and other pieces to articulate the pain and the longing. What if those gifted with the pen could teach and encourage others to recontextualize Psalms, including Psalms of Lament, by having people writing a psalm in their own words in order to express your communal story in order to help people name their pain?

What if those who loved animals looked into ways to provide animal therapy? What if dog owners invited those who are struggling and lonely to enjoy playing with their dogs in the park? There are numerous opportunities within the community if we simply look around and notice what is already there.

8. Look for the passions in your congregation.

In an average church, most people may have little professional training, degree, or experience in healing. However, the divorced young mother of four knows something about pain, as does the survivor of childhood sexual abuse. So does the widow of seventeen years, and the army vet with a PTSD diagnosis. These people are in your congregations. Do you see them?

Several years ago, there was a mother of two in our congregation who was a passionate advocate for the poor and homeless in our community. I wondered where that driving passion for the underprivileged and under-resourced came from; then I heard her story. In her first marriage, she was a victim of domestic abuse. Scared and with a toddler, she felt trapped – until one day, she made the courageous decision to leave the destructive relationship. She and her young daughter lived in her car for eight months. Years later, by God's mercy, she has landed on her feet again. Now, she felt it was her God-given obligation to serve others in similar situations. As she serves, she sees her younger self in their faces and hears her own story as they tell her theirs. She can't *not* be a part of their lives.

These seemingly ordinary (yet truly inspiring) people want to be counted among those bringing healing in the name of Jesus. Unfortunately, they often feel underqualified or disqualified altogether, believing they don't have much to offer. But they *do* have a great deal to offer. In fact, they might even have *the most* to offer. How might we recognize, call out, empower, unleash, release, and celebrate them in their desire to join God's mission?[31] How might their stories be highlighted? Where could we affirm them and then invite them into spaces and opportunities to further steward their wounds for good in the world?

9. Look for the healers within your broader community.

Bringing healing is always a communal venture. We must stand shoulder to shoulder with other leaders in our ZIP codes. As some churches are given some specific *charisms* – gifts from the Holy Spirit – other churches are graciously given different gifts. We often read Paul's metaphorical imagery of the body of Christ myopically. When Paul wrote of the different body parts, he wasn't wanting us to think merely about those in our specific local church (1 Cor. 12:12-31); instead, he desired for God's people to think with a larger more holistic understanding of the body across ZIP codes and denominations, without barriers or borders. One church may be full of healers in one particular area, while another church may be passionate about another expression of healing to address suffering in the community. Are we aware of the gifts each local church around us possesses? And if so, how can we attempt to cultivate a gospel vision for kingdom partnerships to develop for great effectiveness in our communities?

Each church doesn't need to reinvent the wheel, but it does

need to link arms. And each local congregation cannot possibly meet all the needs within a specific community. In trying to do so, the church—its pastors, leaders, and congregants—will be left feeling exhausted, discouraged, disillusioned, and maybe even cynical. No church can bring all the healing a community needs. Yet when churches think strategically, serve radically, and link arms creatively to partner with others, we can bring the healing others are desperately looking for. Local churches, whether large or small, whether residing in an urban, rural, or suburban area, whether serving the affluent or among the poor, have certain gifts and passions entrusted to them. Instead of every other church in your community having their own food pantry, a coordinated effort among several churches together to create a robust, holistic, and synergized food pantry provides more strategic opportunities for service.

My friends, Stuart Davis and Corrie Smith, help lead one of these coordinated kingdom efforts through a faith-based, community-wide, non-profit organization called COSILoveYou whose mission statement is "Unite and ignite the Church to love the city of Colorado Springs." It took years of difficult and patient work to build trust and develop buy-in from dozens of local churches around the city. Now Stuart and Corrie, along with a team of other staff and volunteers, have seen tangible evidence of kingdom collaboration. They connect dots and build bridges between civic officials and local churches who link arms to serve needs and provide healing for their city. They mobilize staff and volunteers through diverse local churches, exhibit selfless and non-territorial leadership, and have developed a clear communication strategy. When COSILoveYou hears of a need in the city, it's passed on to the network of partner churches, who enthusiastically raise their hands and offer to meet the need. When the pandemic hit, a local public health agency identified isolated residents and sent information to COSILoveYou, who mobilized over forty churches to respond by delivering groceries and hygiene products – paid for and dropped off by the churches themselves. COSILoveYou also brought nearly a dozen churches together to fund free weekly lunches at the four major hospitals around the city throughout the summer months, providing fun meals to encourage and support frontline health workers. One church stepped up and funded the purchase of life-saving technology which was desperately needed in one of the hospitals in order to continue treating COVID-19 patients.

Additionally, the organization mobilized over two thousand volunteers to serve in nearly one hundred service projects around the city in groups of ten or less, no strings attached. With the country on lockdown, they hosted virtual gatherings, including a space for city-wide worship led by worship leaders from five different churches and attended by over five hundred people. Another online meeting convened one hundred senior pastors where the main purpose was to discuss the question, "How can the Church become our city's greatest partner and advocate in bringing flourishing to our community?"[32] Each local church realized they couldn't serve all of the needs of their city, but they understood if they stewarded their passions and gifts faithfully, while also linking arms with other churches throughout the city, they could be more strategic and ignite kingdom synergy.

But even beyond churches, how might you look for individuals or organizations who are a part of the healing, even if they have no religious affiliation? There are great non-faith-based organizations in almost every community who are a part of the healing process. Ask yourself this simple question: *when there is great pain, tragedy, or need in your community, where do people immediately think to turn to for help?*

- Where do people look when they are addicted or evicted?

- Where do people go when they are stressed or depressed?
- Where do people look when they need financial assistance?
- Where do people look for help when their home was destroyed by fire, or when they find out their teenager is contemplating suicide?
- Whoever they might turn to, plain and simple: look for ways to partner with them. Call and ask, "How can we link arms and serve?"

10. Look for future healers.

It's also easy to overlook younger generations. We can make the tragic assumption that younger people haven't had enough life experience to know what suffering is really like or, even worse, they don't want to help others. Unfortunately, a significant percentage of people who have experienced pain and suffering have been children and youth. While they need care and healing, part of their own healing may include helping others who are suffering. Who are the middle school, high school, and college students in your midst just waiting to be called off the bench to serve? Don't assume they just want to spend hours each day posting selfies to their social media channels (in fact, studies have shown that the most depressed teens post more selfies in order to gain attention and prove that they matter). Younger generations want to make a difference. They also see first-hand their friends suffering deeply, and they don't always know how to help. Imagine if student ministries across the country exposed students to the *sozo* Jesus and then trained them with practical skills to be missionaries cleverly disguised as bringers of healing in their schools, in their neighborhoods, and among their friends?

But this isn't just for younger generations. Look for lay people of all ages in your congregations who are hungry to help others in the future. Almost anyone can be trained in trauma response. Dr. Phil Monroe, director of the American Bible Society's Trauma Healing Institute, trains people who want to bring healing by addressing trauma. He offers: "The secret ingredient to trauma is social connection. The lack of social connection will most likely increase traumatic symptoms. But when it is present it is often something that ameliorates and erases symptoms."[33] Monroe offers three questions people can ask others who have experienced trauma: *What happened? How did that make you feel? What was the hardest part?* For those who have experienced severe trauma, he offers a fourth: *I'm curious: what helped you survive today?*[34] Then he states: stop talking and just listen. Don't offer advice. Don't sermonize. Just listen. When you do this, people begin to open up and connect. And when deep connection occurs, people begin to experience healing.

Christians through the centuries have risen to the occasion in times of crisis, desperation, pain, and loss. They've run toward the pain, not away from it. Will we join Jesus by serving in his field hospital for the sake of the world?

Chapter 5

How Can We Deepen Our Trust in the Holy Spirit to Guide Us as Healers?

*"Where the Spirit of the Lord is, there is freedom,"
says Paul. And we are most in line with the Spirit, most faithfully obedient, when instead of trying
to manipulate people into faith, we simply live
in that freedom and let the Spirit do the work of
transformation.*
   —MARK GALLI

*You keep track of all my sorrows.
You have collected all my tears in your bottle.
You have recorded each one in your book.*
   —PSALM 56:8 (NLT)

If we're going to be the kinds of people who bring healing in Jesus' name, we're going to have to include more than Jesus in the process.

It is quite ironic, tragic even, how in our pursuit of Jesus we often leave the Holy Spirit out of the equation. We are quick to rely on our experience, strategies, competencies – even on Scripture – and yet ignore the accessible healing power available to us through the Holy Spirit. In previous writings, I've shared that many Christians, especially first world Christians, often have a complicated relationship with the Holy Spirit. Talking about the Spirit – who the Spirit is and what the Spirit is capable of doing – can make us emotional, uncomfortable, defensive, and divisive.

Sadly, it's the way I felt for much of my life. I admit: I was fearful of the Holy Spirit. I understood the Spirit like that socially awkward guy at a party. I know him. In fact, I will acknowledge his presence from far across the room. But I don't want to get too close for fear he might say or do something that will be awkward or embarrassing. Cherith Fee Nordling describes people who believe in the Father and the Son, but minimize the role of the Holy Spirit, as *binitarian Christians.* We give mental ascent to the Trinity, but in reality, trust only two members. I was one of these people. Fortunately, several years ago, through the patient guidance of friends, I was able to understand and know the Spirit as a gift, a guide, a friend, and a helper – just as Jesus promised the Spirit would be. What helped me finally relax was when I understood that everything the Spirit does – *everything* – is an effort to point people toward Jesus.[1]

Why do we need to talk about the Holy Spirit in a book about healing? Because the Trinitarian God often brings healing to us today through the presence and work of the Spirit. If we eliminate the Spirit altogether, we minimize the work and potential of healing that Jesus can do in and through us. We must not only talk about the Spirit; we must also submit to, walk with, believe in, befriend, and relish this wonderful Spirit, one of three fully participating members of the Trinity. If the world is to count us among the healers, we must look to the Triune God – Father, Son, *and* Spirit. Your experience may be similar to mine. Since many of us may have a limited or anemic understanding of the Holy Spirit, let's back up just a bit and look at this from the ground floor. In John 14, Jesus describes the Holy Spirit with the Greek word *parakletos*, which we often translate as paraclete. This is not all that helpful, as paraclete is not a word we use in our everyday language; it still needs further explanation. The word doesn't have a seamless translation to English. It is part teacher, friend, emboldener, and guide who offers encouragement along the journey. Some translate this word as a counselor.

Does the Spirit Still Work Today?

Your theological background often reveals a great deal about what you believe about the Holy Spirit and what you believe the Spirit is capable of doing today. I, along with many others, share the conviction that the same spirit who we read in the book of Acts is also alive and active in the life of the Church today. We may look around North America and see churches in decline and wonder where the Spirit is. Yet when we look around the globe, we see places where the Good News of Jesus is flourishing, expanding, and growing at a significant rate. And if you look carefully at the places where the Church is growing, you will find that it is most often *within churches and denominations that believe in the active work of the Spirit.* I doubt this is mere coincidence.

The charismatic movement has ushered in an undeniable and growing global phenomenon. In fact, charismatic churches are the fastest growing category of churches and denominations in the world, especially in Central and South Americas and Africa. While you may not be a full-blown, card-carrying, hair-on-fire, banner-waving, tambourine-shaking charismatic (I am not), we at least need to pause and reflect upon why there is so much growth among this group of believers. Most pointedly, the charismatic movement is a global healing phenomenon. As Amanda Porterfield wrote in her book *Healing in the History of Christianity,* in Korea, the U.K., Russia, Italy, Brazil, Mexico, Chile, Africa, and Latin America – and parts of North America – the combination of the belief in the literal truth of Scripture, the priority of spiritual gifts, and the centrality of healing with

Jesus as its source is the source of the movement's flourishing.[2]

Healing is at the epicenter of what people in these regions of the world need and desire the most.

Poor health is one of the significant threats to those in poverty. The healing is spiritual, emotional, mental, and also physical. Many American Christians can easily get on board with the first three, but struggle to accept that physical healings still take place today. And yet, there are numerous, frequent, and credible reports coming out of the Global South of physical healing, even reports of people coming back from the dead. Philip Jenkins, professor of history at Baylor University, stated that there is a single word that separates Christians from the Global South and the Global North: *healing*. In the Christian context in the Global North, healing often holds a negative connotation and conjures up images of phony faith healers and televangelists. And yet, Christians in the Global South believe in healing, but they integrate healing of mind, body, spirit, and society.[3]

Of course, there are myriad questions that arise when we hear reports of this nature – and rightfully so. Maybe the most notably: *Why doesn't this happen where I live?* It's a valid question. I won't attempt to answer this question comprehensively, but I have wondered: if we continue to live our lives as if we don't believe (or even desire for this to occur), then maybe God wants to answer the prayers of others who are praying desperately for these sorts of occurrences. Similar to how Christianity thrived in the first few centuries – because of its emphasis on caring for the sick and wounded and offering compassionate healing – charismatic and other Spirit-affirming congregations thrive for many of the same reasons today.[4]

Does it mean that we must all attend a church associated with a denomination that actively affirms the ongoing work of the Spirit in the life of the church? I don't believe so. But it will almost certainly require that we become a charismatic believer – at least in the lowercase *c* sense of charismatic. By charismatic, I mean someone who believes that the Spirit is an active and central member of the Trinity and lives with an active sense of expectation that the Spirit wants to work in the world today to bring about healing.

By God's grace, over the past several years I've experienced noticeable growth in my trust of the Spirit. Now I describe myself as a lowercase *c* charismatic – a charismatic with my seatbelt firmly fastened across my waist. I've found joy, life, freedom, and healing in areas of my life, and I've seen people experience healing because of the Spirit's work. In my journey as a Christian, nothing has freed me (and nothing has made me more uncomfortable) than deepening my trust in the Spirit. Is it awkward at times? Sure. Do I get it right all the time? Of course not. But is there evidence, in my life and the lives of others, of the Spirit's healing, life-giving work? Absolutely. Which makes it completely worth it. And that is the great adventure of following this Triune God. We should not be surprised when what this Spirit-saturated movement offers to the world in Jesus' name is met with evidence of healing in its various forms. Maybe one of the greatest ways we can grow to be people of healing in Jesus' name is to move from being binitarian Christians to Trinitarian Christians.

What Is the Healing Work of the Spirit, and How Can the Spirit Heal in Our Time Today?

In Psalm 51, we read King David pour out his heart in repentance for his sin. David understood that the Spirit played a crucial role in his own restoration. This is significant for us – both in dealing with our sin, but also in our care for others. When we are close to the saving, redeeming, healing nature of the Holy Spirit, we experience renewal.[5]

Pentecost, celebrated each spring as the Spirit's visitation on Christians found in Acts 2, is often referred to as the birthday of the Church. In late May 2020, rioting erupted in many communities across the U.S. in response to racial injustice. Just as the Surgeon General announced the peak of the coronavirus deaths would be on Easter Sunday 2020, riots and looting ripped through cities on Pentecost Sunday. As pastor Rich Villodas wrote,

> *It is symbolically relevant that on Pentecost Sunday, parts of our country were up in flames. Flames of rage, flames of pain, and flames burning for justice. Pentecost is also a day when we remember the flames – but of a different kind. Flames of the Holy Spirit resting on the heads of Jesus' disciples. The flames of the Spirit are given so we can extinguish the flames of injustice.*
>
> *Pentecost is not a day to re-create what happened 2,000 years ago, or manipulate people into a state of mystical ecstasy. Pentecost is not simply a powerful emotional and spiritual experience that enables us to speak in tongues and fall on the floor. Pentecost is about the outpouring of the Holy Spirit. A gift from God, to empower us to cross barriers that are often too thick to break down on our own… Pentecost is our annual reminder that God has given the Church the Holy Spirit, not to satisfy our private, insatiable lust for more experiences, but to mark us as witnesses of Jesus' kingdom. A kingdom marked by love, justice, forgiveness and reconciliation.*[6]

John Wimber, the founder of the Vineyard Movement, wrote that when we partner with the Spirit, everyone gets to play.[7] What a great phrase. *But, you may wonder, if we believe the Spirit's active work today, how might I practically join with the Holy Spirit in an effort to be a healer in Jesus' name?* In Romans 8, Paul outlines for the early Christians in Rome what a believer's relationship to the Holy Spirit looks like. Paul differentiates between a person who lives according to the flesh and a person who lives according to the Spirit. What I find noteworthy is that Paul gives two – and only two – options. He does not include a third category. He holds no category for someone who rejects the flesh, but who is also leery of the Spirit; one who holds a cognitive appreciation for the Spirit, but without any daily, first-hand experience to show. To be a Christian, Paul assumed, was to be a person whose entire outlook was shaped by the Spirit (v. 5). He continues a few verses later: "But if Christ is in you, your body is dead because of sin, but the Spirit is your life because of righteousness" (v. 10). That sounds like healing to me. But Paul gets more specific with this idea of the Spirit providing healing: "For I consider that our present sufferings cannot even be compared to the coming glory that will be revealed to us" (v. 18).

What Makes the Holy Spirit Irreplaceable in the Ministry of Healing?

The work of the Holy Spirit is to reveal the active presence of God in the world. After Jesus ascended into heaven, the Spirit is now the *primary* evidence of the Trinity in the world today.[8] The Spirit's activity was – and continues to be – about *bringing blessing.*[9] And that blessing is expressed in four primary ways: empowering, purifying, revealing, and unifying. When the Spirit *empowers,* he gives life.[10] He also empowers people to serve in the name of Jesus.[11] When the Spirit *purifies*, he is setting us apart to be used as people of blessing in the world.[12] When the

Spirit *reveals,* he gives noticeable evidence so others can see God at work. He guides and directs us to know how and where and to whom to be people of blessing and healing.[13] When the Spirit *unifies,* he mends, reconciles, brings together those who have been broken, divided, and apart – all works of healing.[14]

In addition to providing comfort and health, the purposes of healing are to reveal evidence of God's work to verify his blessing in the world and give further opportunity for people to see and experience the goodness and graciousness of a loving Father.[15] We see evidence of the early Church being filled with or baptized by the Spirit.[16] For some of us, when we read about the baptism of the Holy Spirit, it may sound confusing or come with its own set of religious baggage.[17] But based on what we see in these fillings, they were equipped and empowered to be healers. Therefore, continuing in the long line of faith-filled people in our family tree, we should ask for this filling in our lives. Receiving such a filling will enable and empower us to be people of blessing and healing like we see with the early disciples.[18] Being filled is not a one-time event; instead, it is an ongoing process. Just like a pitcher filled with water, being filled with the Spirit allows us to be ready and able to be tipped over and poured out into others at any moment. Being filled makes us more like Christ and gives us an increase in power for spiritual gifts to be used – not for our own pride, but so that Jesus can be seen, responded to, and praised.[19] Sometimes that Spirit-induced healing occurred by laying on of hands.[20] Other times through the anointing with oil.[21]

Paul and Peter give us several lists of spiritual gifts in the New Testament.[22] Among two of those lists is the gift of healing. Some of you reading this book may be entrusted with the gift of healing. If so, you have a special responsibility to steward it well. But to the rest of us, we're not off the hook. While gifts may vary in strength and expression, it does not mean that God can't – or won't – use you to provide some element of healing to people's lives. While the Spirit most often hands out gifts which are permanent in a person's life, let us not believe, even for a moment, that people are "stuck" with certain gifts and not with others. Remember, the Spirit is a part of the Trinity, who moves and acts as he pleases for his glory.

Spirit-empowered healing is not a mindless, predictable, paint-by-numbers approach. No healthy relationship is, of course. But there are specific ways and postures in which we can submit to and join with the Spirit as healers.

First, w*e must let the Spirit be the Spirit and stop being so afraid of awkwardness.*

Until we let go of the awkwardness we feel and the baggage we may have regarding the Spirit, we will always have a stilted and strained relationship with the Trinity. Maybe our first act of trust is to ask boldly for freedom from any awkwardness, baggage, pain, misunderstanding, uneasiness around who the Spirit actually is. We may also need to ask for forgiveness for how we've allowed the fear of others to dominate where we've resisted participating with the Spirit.

Second*, we can pray specifically for the Spirit to be present, recognized, trusted – and enjoyed.*

Earlier we mentioned Luke's unique perspective as both a physician and a gospel writer. In addition to healing, prayer is also a key theme that runs throughout his gospel. To Luke, healing and prayer go together. I am convinced that if Luke were here among us today, he would have a hard time believing we could be healers in the name of Jesus without an ever-deepening and ongoing life of prayer.

We can – and *should* – pray for healing in ourselves and in others. Wayne Grudem points out that if we tell people God seldom heals today and that they shouldn't expect healing to occur, it stunts our faith and cuts off an opportunity for God to be honored and glorified. This is far from what we see in the New Testament. However, if we tell people that God always heals people if we "just have more faith," we can wound people even more deeply. Grudem states that we must live in the tension with wisdom, residing somewhere between the extremes.[23]

If the Spirit is our helper and emboldener, can we not ask the Spirit to help us and embolden us in the process? Paul continued: "In the same way, the Spirit helps us in our weakness, for we do not know how we should pray, but the Spirit himself intercedes for us with inexpressible groanings. And he who searches our hearts knows the mind of the Spirit, because the Spirit intercedes on behalf of the saints according to God's will" (Rom. 8:27).

How might we pray specifically?

We should pray for our own healing. And invite others into the process, too.

We can start by asking the Spirit to provide healing for us. James wrote specifically and pointedly to this end: "Are any of you sick? You should call for the elders of the church to come and pray over you, anointing you with oil in the name of the Lord" (Jas. 5:14). We need the soothing salve from *Christus medicus.* We are all broken; our human limitations remind us of our frailty. When we pray – and invite others to pray – for our healing, and it happens, it is reason to celebrate. It also makes us bolder, more confident, and more comfortable to ask the Spirit for healing on behalf of others in the ministry of healing.

We embrace what the Spirit can do through us in the lives of other people.

Lailah Gifty Akita wrote, "Without the Helper, there is no help." We can also begin to pray – specifically and boldly – that God would equip us to become helpers and healers who represent him appropriately as his hands and feet. And can ask, with equal measures of faith-filled humility and bold confidence, that God would work through our words, our eyes, our mind, our ears, our tongues, and our touch to bring healing to others. Yes, it is God who does the healing, not us, but we can pray he uses us to become a conduit of his healing *through* our lives and *into* others.

We can commit to praying regularly and *specifically* for those who are in need of healing. Unfortunately, we often pray for healing in general terms:
- *Lord, if it is your will, would you heal Lisa?*
- *Holy Spirit, bring about your healing touch on Larry's body right now in his cancer treatments...*
- *God, you know better than we do, but please work in the life of the Edmondson family...*
- *Lord, bring about healing to the people in South America who have experienced a major tragedy this week...*

These prayers are not inherently bad; they are just not the kinds of powerful prayers healers are permitted to pray. The Spirit invites us into prayer *with specificity* for Lisa and Larry and the Edmondsons and the devastation of the natural disaster in South America. Should we make demands of God when we pray? No. But should we preface our prayers and keep to generalities, to give ourselves a way out if our petition goes unanswered? No. Prefacing and speaking in generalities can often be a sneaky way in which we hedge our bets in order to keep ourselves from potential disappointment when God does not act the way we desire in the timeframe we want. Most often, fear of disappointment has kept countless Christians from praying with boldness and specificity. We should attempt to make up God's mind for him. Let us pray boldly, and let him decide if and how he works in the situation. What if we grew to trust God – even with our potential disappointment of a lack of results in healing – in order to pray with boldness and faith?

Maybe when we pray, we receive a word which was downloaded into our minds and hearts by God. Sharing that appropriately, wisely, compassionately, and boldly with someone else can bless them. Laying hands on someone's ailing knee and asking for God to work boldly is how healers pray. Interceding on behalf of someone else who has been deeply wounded can lead to creative ways to bless someone in the name of Jesus. Even if it does not *cure* them fully, it can *provide healing* that is nonetheless meaningful, important, and freeing. When we pray as Spirit-oriented healers, we invite the Spirit to do what only the Spirit can do. That is the point of healing prayer.

If the world is to look to us to provide healing in Jesus' name, we must look to the Triune God – Father, Son, and Spirit.

Chapter 6

How Can We Be Prepared to Be Bringers of Healing?

Our job is to be a presence, rather than a savior, a companion, rather than a leader, a friend, rather than teacher.
   —**JOHN WELSHONS**, *AWAKENING FROM GRIEF*

There is a time for everything,
and a season for every activity under the heavens:
a time to be born and a time to die,
a time to plant and a time to uproot,
a time to kill and a time to heal…
   —**ECCLESIASTES 3:1-3A**

Ernest Hemingway's short story, "The Capital of the World," centers around the life of a young man named Paco. Set in Madrid, Paco spends his days as a waiter, but longs to become a matador one day. In a heated exchange, he wrongs his father, and, in his shame, he runs away. His father, in an attempt to reconcile with his estranged son, searches tirelessly for him all over Spain to no avail. In a desperate attempt to find him, he places a prominent ad in the Madrid newspaper.

> PACO,
> MEET ME AT THE
> HOTEL MONTAÑA.
> NOON TUESDAY.
> ALL IS FORGIVEN.
> -PAPA

When the father arrives at the hotel at noon on Tuesday, he is astonished at what he finds: eight hundred Pacos, all looking for their father.[1] The world is desperately longing for someone to welcome them home.

But longing for connection and actually forging those bonds are two separate things. The woundedness many have endured, especially in the midst of a pandemic, has damaged the connective tissue to such a fragile state. Reconnecting that tissue requires vulnerability, tenderness, patience, and compassion, which involves personal inner work before we can move out to serve others.

Wearing Masks – and Discarding Others

Before 2020, most Americans had never worn a surgical mask. Within months, we were all wearing them. When the coronavirus first tore through the U.S., many of us remember that hospitals and medical professionals were in desperate need of N95 masks and other personal protective equipment. As the forest fires raged out west in the fall of 2020, residents wore masks not just to protect against the virus, but also to protect against the hazardous air quality. We grew accustomed to wearing masks (well, most of us).[2] Masks were no longer reserved for just medical professionals; they're for all of us.

Yet if we're going to help with the healing, we're going to have to put on another kind of mask as well: an oxygen mask. We've all heard the spiel given on every domestic flight: *in the unlikely event of an emergency, put your mask on first before assisting others.* As healers, we must make sure we strap our masks tightly across our face and breathe in the air of the Spirit.[3] We offer ourselves in service to others in the new reality with the call to take up the oxygen mask. It is impossible to be the faithful, compassionate, and caring healers over the long haul if we are not inhaling the life-giving breath of the Spirit on a daily basis. Attempting to be bringers of healing in our own strength, without the crucial life source of the Holy Spirit, will actually makes us ineffective at best, and spiritually dead at worst.

In picking up our literal masks and our figurative oxygen masks, we will need to put down other masks we may have been wearing for years. We must drop our mask of pretention. In order to be healers, we must bring our true selves to the process and have the courage to be authentic. We must drop our mask of expertise and know-how. Hurting people are not looking for brilliance; they are looking for presence, connection, and compassion. Despite our best intentions, if we mix up which masks to pick up and which to cast aside, we will, in all likelihood, cause more harm than good.

Facing a World Filled with Pain

If we want to be healers, we must understand our own limitations. Wounded healers must be aware of the real hazard of burnout. Burnout can be described as numbness, apathy – even resentment or anger – toward a situation, toward God, or toward people. It's where we lose our joy, our passion, our first love. There are so many needs, so many wounded souls, so much that needs to be addressed. Compassion fatigue is real, and burnout is a risk in the lives of those who desire to bring healing.

How can we possibly address all the needs we see around us? We can't. First, we must understand our limitations – that we can't possibly meet every need, even if we spent the rest of our days trying. This is a hard reality, but it is an important truth we must accept. The greatest element of our faith expressed as healers may not be when we serve others, but instead when we refrain from serving others and letting God do his work. We must not allow ourselves to believe that we are ultimately the solution to the problems around us. Sometimes, the healthiest thing we can do is say no.

Burnout is present when boundaries are absent. Constantly saying yes will ultimately kill us in the end. It's crucial we realize that Jesus didn't address every issue or heal every person he came in contact with. There were still large amounts of infirmities, demonic possession, and death in Galilee and Jerusalem despite the presence of his ministry. Third, when we are feeling the effects of burnout, we must name it and share it appropriately with others. And when we name it, we need to take a real break, take time to heal, process it with others, and then create healthy boundaries and expectations before re-entry. Despite the best intentions, wounded healers who experience burnout and refuse to address its effects create more wounds, for themselves and others.

If we want to be healers, we must lean into difficult conversations about American culture. The world watched in horror as George Floyd's life was squeezed out of him by the knee of a Minneapolis police officer for almost nine minutes. But there were many others whose lives have ended – or been altered – tragically. Racial tensions across the country – and across the world – swelled, leading to protests and rallies lamenting the unnecessary loss of life, highlighting the injustices against people of color, and pushing for reform in various areas. The Church must acknowledge there is racial trauma which many people of color have experienced – not just recently, but for centuries. Will the Church stand by and watch passively and idly? Will most Christians nod passively in agreement yet refuse to roll up our sleeves and get involved? Or will the church be a part of the messy, uncomfortable, and significant work of redemption, reconciliation, and forgiveness?

Unfortunately, the discussion of racial justice and equality has become extremely emotional and unequivocally political. But to love our neighbor as ourselves, to care for the oppressed, to stand up for those whose voices have been silenced or muted is not a political decision, but a kingdom one (Mic. 6:8, Prov. 31:8-9). Writing as a white male, it is crucial for me to simultaneously stand up for those who are oppressed, while also exhibiting meekness by listening – *really* listening – to what people of color have experienced and continue to experience frequently. It's difficult to help people heal from trauma when we're always doing the talking. So much of the racial tension, especially for majority white leaders and churches, means showing up and shutting up. For wounds to heal, people need to know they matter. And in order to communicate that people truly matter, it will mean that we become people who are committed to truly listening to those who've been hurt by the racial trauma.

If we are going to take up the call to be bringers of healing in Christ's name, we must move toward the pain.

If we want to be healers, we must understand the trauma others are facing. We touched on trauma earlier, but it's worth revisiting here. The widespread trauma, in its various forms—matched with chronic loneliness and isolation—provides a significant opportunity for the Church to bring healing. In people's trauma, we must ensure that we attend to people's woundedness, where we hold space for God to bring the healing balm of his touch in their lives. We cannot fix trauma, but we can serve as sacred space-holders.

Maybe most devastating of all trauma is childhood trauma. Frequently, severe loneliness often begins with some level of trauma during the important developmental years in childhood.

Domestic violence, gang violence, murder, divorce, and abandonment seldom make for happy childhoods and healthy kids. These early-stage wounds can leave scars which last their entire lives.[4] Health experts refer to childhood trauma as adverse childhood experiences (ACEs). This includes physical, emotional, and sexual abuse; physical and emotional neglect; alcoholic parents or a victim of domestic violence; a close family member in jail; or diagnosed with a mental illness. High levels of toxic stress from these situations without the buffer of loving relationships can damage the neurostructural function and development of a child's brain.[5] But there is good news: research shows us that oftentimes a child needed only one loving person in their life to be able to overcome their trauma and experience healing. One loving adult to be both nurturing and emotionally available, mature, and stable – *just one.*[6] How will the Church help people – especially children – work through and heal from trauma?

As well-respected Christian psychologist and leading trauma expert Dr. Diane Langberg shared, "Trauma is the mission field of our time." Old paradigms about missions leads us to think of work on another continent, somewhere overseas, but this new reality reminds us the mission field is in our neighborhood, sometimes under our own roof. If the Church can link arms and show radical love and compassion to those who have experienced trauma, it has the potential to provide so much healing.

If we want to be healers, we must help people heal from chronic loneliness, isolation, and disconnection. Yuval Levin, in his book *A Time To Build,* wrote, "If any single term can describe the ethos of our time, the very age in which social media has flowered, it would be isolation."[7] Even before the coronavirus, our world was also already experiencing a loneliness epidemic, what Mother Teresa called the leprosy of the modern world.[8]

U.S. Surgeon General, Dr. Vivek Murthy, called loneliness a public health crisis.[9]

In the introduction to his book, *Together: The Human Power of Connection in a Sometimes Lonely World*, he addressed the severity of the issue:

> *To my surprise, the topic of emotional well-being, in general, and loneliness in particular, receive the strongest response from the public of any issues I worked on as Surgeon General. There were a few issues that elicited as much enthusiastic interest from both very conservative and very liberal members of Congress, from young and old people, or from urban and rural arrested and so like.... It's a universal condition that affects all of us directly or through the people we love.*[10]

The Centers for Disease Control and Prevention report reveals that suicide rates across the country have increased by almost 30 percent over the past two decades.[11] The increase has been particularly steep in rural America and along the so-called Rust Belt, from parts of Appalachia to the upper Midwest. In the same regions, life expectancy has actually been going down. Additionally, opioid abuse is often found amidst deep isolation, desperation, and misery.[12] Countless people live their days addicted to these drugs – alive, but barely. Opioids are used to dull pain, not sharpen experience; its primary use is to *escape suffering*.[13] These so-called "deaths of despair" have led to a dip in life expectancy – the first sustained decline since the time of World War I and the Spanish flu.[14] This should alarm us all. Is the Church in North America paying attention to such things?

Eric Kleinenberg, in his book *Heat Wave,* looked at the devastating heat wave that hit Chicago for a week in mid-July 1995. Temperatures reached 106 degrees, with a heat index of 126. It buckled streets, shut down the city's power grids, leaving residents without electricity for several days. By the end of the week, more than seven hundred residents had died. For perspective, this was twice as many as had died in the Great Chicago Fire of 1871.[15] Kleinenberg learned that the vast majority of those who passed away were elderly and poor residents who died in their places of residence alone. No one checked on them; they had no one to care for them when heat stroke set in. They died of loneliness.[16] While social distancing can help mitigate a viral pandemic, too much social distancing ushers in another kind of devastating pandemic altogether.

God has wired us for connection, which is the foundation of healing. Emotional and relational (and sometimes physical) healing happens when we are known, cared for, and loved by others – the power of true community. Maybe one of the most practical ways churches can serve their communities is to create a hotline where lonely people can call if they simply need someone to talk to. Churches can coordinate times and train volunteers to listen and befriend people who desperately long for connection. What are the creative and compassionate expressions of love the church can help those who have experienced chronic loneliness, isolation, and disconnection?

If we want to be healers, we must walk with people in their anxiety and loss. As stated earlier, the state of people's mental health has already been fragile – especially those who were already vulnerable *before* COVID-19. Therapists and researchers warned of a "perfect storm" of suicide risk factors: economic stress, isolation, low community support, limited treatment access, nationwide anxiety, and booming gun sales.[17] A mental health crisis helpline saw a spike in calls during national lockdown of almost nine times the normal volume.[18] Due to this ongoing nationwide increase, the National Suicide Hotline Designation Act was signed into law in the fall of 2020; by July 2022, it will allow those experiencing a mental health emergency or suicidal ideation to simply dial 988 to connect with a crisis center specialist.[19] How will the Church respond to the anxiety and loss people have experienced?

If we want to be healers, we must prioritize healing in our church ministries. Earlier we explored Jesus' ministry expressed in three primary ways: preaching, teaching, healing.[20] Many pastors and church leaders go to seminary to become great preachers and teachers, but few enroll in seminary in order to become better healers. The Church in North America has been known for its preaching and teaching ministries, but only on rare occasion is it known for its healing ministry. My friend Janet Durrwachter, a Methodist pastor, shared that the church often values teaching and preaching because these are the domains of the pastor as a trained professional. If a church has a healing ministry, it is all too often relegated to a retired pastor who does hospital visits and weekly home visitations. Those on the top of the org chart always preach but rarely are in primary roles of healing. But in this new reality, the opportunity is ripe for those values to shift: what if the highest priority of a local church was for a healing ministry – and then teaching and preaching?

When people experience bombs of destruction, we can bring a balm of healing. Look around. There are Pacos everywhere. Are we prepared to help them?

Chapter 7

What Are the Marks of Wounded Healers?

When the tears come streaming down your face
When you lose something you can't replace
When you love someone but it goes to waste
Could it be worse?
—COLDPLAY, "FIX YOU"

To this you were called, because Christ suffered for you, leaving you an example, that you should follow in his steps.
—1 PETER 2:21

In my first ministry position, I served as the pastor of college and young adults at a large church in Colorado. Four adventure-loving twenty-somethings from our ministry spent an afternoon enjoying the beautiful outdoors rock climbing in the famous Garden of the Gods Park in Colorado Springs, just a few miles from the church campus. Before beginning the route, the four young men safely secured their harnesses, ropes, and safety clips in place. During one climb, on one of the well-used climbing routes, one of the young men's foot slipped suddenly. Despite the safety clips being installed correctly, the red rock formations throughout the park had become brittle due to uncharacteristically heavy and frequent summer rains and crumbled, forcing the rock to break apart and the safety clip to spring free. The rope intended to break his fall did not. The young man plunged off the cliff and landed just feet away from his three climbing friends. Unconscious, he was rushed to the emergency room.

My phone rang shortly thereafter updating me of the news. I dropped everything, grabbed the keys to my Jeep, and rushed to the hospital unsure if he would be alive when I arrived. As I charged into the emergency room waiting area, I noticed dozens of anxious and crying friends and families from the church huddled together. Another pastor on our staff approached, informing me that, just a moment prior, the young man had been pronounced dead. The pastor ushered me to the door of the grieving room to provide comfort to his three friends who were waiting inside. These three friends had witnessed his fall in front of their very eyes and now had just learned of his death a moment prior.

As I entered the room, I saw the three lying on the floor in a heap of immense pain. They were lying on top of each other, their eyes closed, shaking uncontrollably, wailing in deep anguish, unable to process their trauma of what they had just seen. They heaved, as snot and tears fell off their faces and onto the carpet. Years later, I can still hear the sound of their wailing and sobbing in my mind.

The Marks of Wounded Healers

In the ancient world, the expectations God placed upon healers were quite unique. As we read in Exodus and Leviticus, priests from the line of Aaron were required to engage in specific and meticulous ceremonial practices: washing, inspecting, splattering blood on the horns of the altar, burning contaminated clothes – even social distancing and week-long quarantines. A priest was, in essence, a combination of spiritual mediator, religious dermatologist, health inspector, and ceremonial grill master. While many of these cultural practices may leave us scratching our heads, for the nation of Israel, it was a severe act of God's mercy as it helped them to avoid plagues, diseases, and epidemics that had the potential to wipe out their entire nation.

But what are the markers of healers in our current context? If the world is looking for healers, what identifiable evidence exists today? If we take our *Sozo* Mandate seriously, wounded healers must embody and exhibit eight significant marks.[1]

Mark #1: Wounded healers bear scars and offer them to others as a source of identity, solidarity, and vulnerability.

The world has experienced the universality of woundedness and trauma. As Mako Fujimura stated, it became our "universal connective tissue."[2] As we've looked at before, scars were the primary physical marks of following a risen, wounded, yet victorious savior. There is no such thing as a scar-free healer. Yet there is a strong temptation to ignore, hide, or minimize our own scars.

We must embrace our own weaknesses and limitations. When we have the grace and the courage to acknowledge our wounds, it builds trust with those we lead and serve. It announces, *I am with you. I can relate to your pain. I, too, have been wounded. I, too, am stumbling toward the great Wounded Healer.* Paul, in his introductory remarks to the church in Corinth, offers this emphasis of shared suffering while pointing to Christ, our healer and comforter:

> *God is our merciful Father and the source of all comfort. He comforts us in all our troubles so that we can comfort others. When they are troubled, we will be able to give them the same comfort God has given us. For the more we suffer for Christ, the more God will shower us with his comfort through*

> *Christ. Even when we are weighed down with troubles, it is for your comfort and salvation! For when we ourselves are comforted, we will certainly comfort you. Then you can patiently endure the same things we suffer. We are confident that as you share in our sufferings, you will also share in the comfort God gives us. (2 Cor. 1:3-7 NLT)*

As we touch our own wounds and name our own pain, we are often invited by others to lovingly and gently touch their pain. It is what expands and deepens trust and earns the right to address – and dress – their wounds. It is from this starting point wounded healers can be motivated by compassion and mercy. Compassion, in the original Latin root, means "co-suffering." When we love well, we suffer alongside of others.

Mark #2: Wounded healers are rooted in a robust theology of suffering and of hope.

As we touched on earlier in the book, wounded healers cannot encourage others to simply move on without first grieving the loss. To encourage people to have more faith or just get over it is, at least, stunting their growth and shutting down trust—if not wounding them further.[3] We may say all the right things. We may quote Scripture. We may remind them of the goodness of God. We may tell others there is meaning in their pain. And while these may be true, it is not the whole truth, for they are still in their suffering. If we are tempted to rush the healing process too quickly, we can end up sounding like a flimsy Christian sympathy card. We may be tempted to prescribe answers for God's work; our intentions may be pure, but we end up wounding even more. We cannot grow impatient with the healing process, for the process usually takes longer than we would desire.

But the inefficiency of healing is where our faith is tested. In the vast majority of cases, healing does not occur overnight. It's an excruciatingly slow process.

We also must not be shocked when suffering occurs. Wounded healers acknowledge this is an unavoidable part of the human condition, as Jesus told his followers. "In this world you will have trouble and suffering…" (Jn. 16:33 NLT). I wonder if Jesus is shocked by our shock that suffering occurs. Left to itself, Jesus' word seems hopeless and nihilistic. But Jesus finished by saying, "…but take courage – I have conquered the world" (33b NET). We live in the tension: yes, suffering exists. No, we are not without help or hope. Wounded healers help others realize that growth and maturity cannot occur without first healthily entering into grief. If we can help others grasp that if they are willing to climb into the dark caves of their pain, they will find Jesus waiting there with his arms wide open.

Mark #3: Wounded healers work toward forgiveness and help others enter into the messy process of forgiveness.

Many of the wounds people possess are rooted in relational and emotional pain. Bitterness can easily set in; this unfulfilled revenge can be destructive to the soul. Resentment is nothing more than marinated unforgiveness. And yet, forgiveness is the DNA of the *sozo* Jesus. The Lord's Prayer, our pledge of allegiance of God's people, has forgiveness written into it. As Bernard of Clairvaux wrote, "If God had not loved his enemies he would have no friends." As Catholic theologian Ronald Rolheiser wrote, "Any pain or tension that we do not transform we will transmit. In the face of jealousy, anger, bitterness, and hatred we must be like water purifiers, holding the poisons and toxins inside of us and giving back just the pure water, rather than being like electrical cords that simply pass on the energy that flows through them." Many books have been written on the healing power of forgiveness. We do not have time to unpack fully the work of forgiveness and its close cousin, reconciliation. And yet, our role as wounded healers is to enter into the difficult and messy work of moving toward forgiveness and helping others do the same, for in forgiveness we find true healing. It is the gospel story. When we forgive and help others do the same, we are enacting the gospel, and we become agents of *sozo* in the world.

Rolheiser again:

> *As we age, we can begin to trim down our spiritual vocabulary, and eventually we can get it down to three words: Forgive, forgive, forgive!... The major task, psychological and spiritual, for the second half of life is to forgive: we need to forgive those who have hurt us, forgive ourselves for our own failings, forgive life for not being fully fair, and forgive God for seemingly being so indifferent to our wounds. We need to do that before we die because ultimately there is only one moral imperative: not to die an angry, bitter person, but to die with a warm heart.*

Mark #4: Wounded healers are committed to engaging in lament, as well as awareness and gratitude.

Lament, simply put, is godly complaint. It is bringing words before God which acknowledge we don't like the space we are in and we long for deliverance and justice. It is where we let it all hang out before God. It is, like Psalm 73 is translated in The Message, *God, are you out to lunch?*[4] It is not a temper tantrum; instead, it is a passionate complaint attached to hope and trust that God is good, powerful, and in control of his world. The African American church has known lament and have prayed collective prayers of lament through the ages.

We cannot have a robust and accurate Christian theology of suffering outside of lament. When we embrace lament, we begin to understand its important part in the healing process. Even Jesus offered prayers of lament: "My God, my God, why have you abandoned me?" (Mt. 27:46 NLT). In such intense and unimaginable pain and suffering, it may be best simply to pray this question-oriented prayer of Jesus with others.

Lament is the language of the new reality. It precedes celebration; it cannot be rushed, manipulated, or contrived. Upon hearing the news of King Saul's death, David wrote a lament – and commanded the entire nation of Israel to know it as well (2 Sam. 1:19-27). Nearly one-third of the psalms are categorized as Lament. The Psalms are the prayer book of the Church, and the Psalms of Lament are training wheels attached to raw and honest prayers, teaching us how to talk honestly and courageously with God. They are liberating; they give us permission and remind us that God is capable of hearing and handling our rated-R prayers. While there are some exceptions, most lament psalms often contain a simple three-part structure: complaint (*"How long, Lord?"*), petition (*"Lord, would you…?"*), and resolution, (*"Yet, you…"*).[5]

Ironically, it is lament that thrusts us forward toward hope. Lament states, *I don't like this, God, but I trust you know about this and you will act redemptively in the future.* We find healthy tension in lament: to only express lament would eventually leave us feeling hopeless and anemic; to only declare praise and gratitude would be to ignore or minimize the pain.

My friend Jared Mackey, a pastor in Denver, offered me three questions to help process such unusual, uncertain, and unprecedented times.

- *What has this painful situation taken away from you today?*

- *What has this painful situation not taken away from you today?*
- *What has this painful situation given to you today?*

The first question is an expression of lament: holy complaint before God and others.

The second is an expression of awareness: an attentiveness to what still remains, even in suffering.

And the third is an expression of gratitude: a vision of new opportunities and blessings present or emerging.

Lament, awareness, and gratitude directed toward God and others can become a redemptive framework for our healing.

Mark #5: Wounded healers refuse to try to fix people.

They are wise enough to know their primary task is not to try to fix others, but to offer hope, presence, and guidance in their healing. Despite our purest of intentions, we cannot fix people, no matter how hard we may try. And we would be wise to make a commitment to refuse to attempt to fix anyone again. As much as we'd like to take away the pain and suffering in someone's life, it ultimately won't occur until Jesus returns and makes all things new. Instead, we can journey with them to mend and attend. We can behold and show honor and dignity to their wounds—physical, emotional, mental, sexual, financial, relational, racial, and spiritual.

We attend to others' pain, but the moment we attempt to fix them, we run the serious and damaging risk of inflicting more pain and wounds. Harold Senkbeil wrote:

> *A true physician of souls is not a soothsayer or medium. We never attempt to read the tea leaves of tragedy or mayhem here in this world to discover the hidden meaning behind them. The fact is that we*

human beings are unable to discern God's disposition by decoding the events in a person's life… Sometimes the only comfort we have to bring is this: we have a suffering God.[6]

Fixing puts us in a position of power, where we are easily seduced into thinking we can play God. It demeans others and provides distance to the relationship. It's dangerous. Instead, we are to be present and attentive, to behold and to bear their pain with them as we journey toward a Jesus who wants to make us new. Don't fix; just provide space for connection.

Mark #6: Wounded healers courageously and compassionately listen and ask questions.

As Senkbeil also wrote, that offering healing means we pay attention in Jesus' name.[7] It is hurtful when others attempt to prescribe, explain, diagnose, or speak for God in the midst of our pain. What we need most in those moments is not an insightful answer, but a soothing presence. Wounded healers refuse to presume to know what people's wounds are or how to fix them. Offering answers – even the *theologically correct* answers – can be perceived as a form of control; asking questions can be a way of releasing control and offering dignity to those who are hurting.

What I find so astounding is Jesus—despite being fully God—asked questions. Lots of them. Jesus asked over three hundred questions in the Gospels. It wasn't that he needed more information. To Jesus, questions were a form of compassion and care. Jesus, the wounded healer, asked questions—even when he already knew the answers—*because questions are one of the most important forms of connection in all of the human experience.* Questions are gifts wounded healers can give those who long for healing. Questions rarely take away the pain; but they can provide help to endure. Christianity is far from the only religion to take healing seriously. In fact, almost all of the world's major religions do. But part of the appeal is that Christianity helps us understand that our suffering is not meaningless.[8]

Wounded healers don't control the process; they submit the journey to the Lord and only join the wounded if they are invited. They do not force their way in. Some questions must be asked for information: *How are you? Where are you suffering? How is your level of pain and suffering today?* But the best questions go deeper and lean into greater vulnerability: *What is it you long for right now? What lies are you tempted to believe through this process – and what truth do you desire to replace it? If you could ask God any questions or share any thoughts with him, what might you say? How can I best serve and support you right now?* Questions open up space, build and strengthen the bridge of trust, and invite others closer. The best questions can tend to the presence of Christ in a hospital room, over the phone, on the front porch, or over a cup of coffee. When the right questions are asked at the right time for the right reason, healing often follows.

But wounded healers do more than just ask; they also listen. They wait patiently. They offer a full-bodied yes. Many times, this listening seems astoundingly inefficient. But with hope, patience, and faith, in due time it leads to the experience of resurrection.

Mark #7: Wounded healers offer their presence.

As I stood in the grief room looking at those three grieving young men who had just learned of the death of their friend, I was at a loss of what to do or say. I had been in ministry for only about a year and had never been in a pastoral situation like that before. Ill-equipped and uncertain of what to do in such an intense moment, I froze. I listened to their sobs, their tears, their gasps for air.

In that moment, I sensed the strong prompting from the Spirit: *Go lay on top of them.* I knew two of the three, but not closely. As strange and odd as the prompting was, I had no other viable option in that moment. I walked slowly across the room and laid on top of the pile of these young men. I wept with them. Minutes passed. In the darkness of that horrific grief, nobody had yet uttered a word. As I laid on top of them, my mind raced as I pondered what I should say. Nothing came. I was stupefied; I felt incapable, unqualified, completely incompetent. *Pastors are supposed to say something important, something comforting, something spiritual, in moments like this,* I thought. But I had nothing. I just laid prostrate on top of their mournful bodies in silence. And then, after what seemed like ten or fifteen minutes, still without a word, I got up, slowly walked out of the room, and shut the door behind me. In the midst of my own grief, I also felt shameful. In one of the most significant opportunities of my pastoral calling, I had failed miserably.

Or so I thought. During the funeral service, the young man in that grieving room in the ER – the one whom I did not know – shared a story of his friend's life. He was strong and articulate, speaking honoring words of his beloved friend. After the funeral concluded, I approached him to affirm him and also to offer my heartfelt apology for failing to provide comforting words he and his friends would most like have expected in that moment.

But before I could open my mouth he said, "Thank you for laying on top of us the other day in that room in the ER. That's exactly what we needed. And thank you for not saying anything. If you would have spoken, you would have ruined it." I was stunned. Somehow the Spirit had taken what I originally believed to be a colossal pastoral failure and used it for good. All I had to offer was my presence, my own wounds, weakness, sadness, shock, and loss. And somehow these were what the Spirit used in that moment.

Wounded healers embody faithful and hopeful presence. Technology is important and has many benefits, but nothing can replace the importance of incarnational presence with those who are hurting. Jesus came, not as an email or a social media post, but in the flesh – God as a human among other human beings. Wounded healers understand the significance of incarnational presence in the healing process. Simply by showing up, giving our full attention, care, and concern to others can be much-needed salve. You don't have to lay on top of others, but your proximity and presence does matter.

Mark #8: Wounded healers realize they play a part, but ultimately know that true healing is rooted in the love and power of God.

For those who have grown up in environments of deep loss, pains, wounds, and trauma, it can be very difficult for people to trust that God can be good and loving. Dallas Willard wrote, "Never believe anything bad about God." Our sacred role is to share, remind, and point people in the direction of the goodness of God. It is in grasping the goodness and the depth of love God has for people that the healing process begins.

Wounded healers know the power of presence in healing, but also know it is the presence of Christ, the Wounded Healer, who is what the world needs most. We join with God, but we do not play God. During Lent each year, our church invites people to create an art piece and display it during our Good Friday experience. A few years ago, I submitted a piece titled, "Jesus, Our Wounded Healer," in which I took a crucifix, covered the cross with band-aids, and replaced the sign above Jesus' head with a pharmacist's prescription slip. I placed the crucifix on a stone tile and affixed various items from our medicine cabinet to it: ripped gauze pads, used syringes, lozenge wrappers, empty medicine bottles, and old boxes of anti-diarrheal medicine. And before I submitted it, I took a sewing needle, pricked my index finger and dripped blood all over the piece. Under the piece, I included two passages:

> *When Jesus came into Peter's house, he saw Peter's mother-in-law lying in bed with a fever. He touched her hand and the fever left her, and she got up and began to wait on him. When evening came, many who were demon-possessed were brought to him, and he drove out the spirits with a word and healed all the sick. This was to fulfill what was spoken through the prophet Isaiah: "He took up our infirmities and bore our diseases." (Mt. 8:14-17 NIV)*

> *It was our sickness he carried; it was our disease that weighed him down. And we thought his troubles were a punishment from God, a punishment for our own sins! But he was pierced for our rebellion, crushed for our sins. He was beaten so we could be whole. He was whipped so we could be healed. (Is. 53:4-5 NLT)*

Jesus, our wounded healer, invites us to be healed – and then invites us to be the tangible expression of good news in the world. And when we faithfully live into our *Sozo* Mandate, as the world looks around, it will identify us as the healers. And we will have the opportunity to say: *No, it is not us. It is him. Let us experience his healing together.*

Chapter 8

What Is the Connection Between Leadership and Healing?

I am convinced that the Christian leader of the future is called to be completely irrelevant and to stand in this world with nothing to offer but his or her own vulnerable self.
—HENRI NOUWEN

The leader has a special responsibility to pay attention to what's happening inside of himself or herself, lest the act of leadership do more harm than good.
—PARKER PALMER

On March 11, 2011, an earthquake hit off the shore of Japan – the most powerful in the nation's history. Its tremors created a massive tsunami which pummeled the country and swept over its shores almost six miles inland. Entire communities were wiped out, cars floated down streets, and people were left homeless. Over fifteen thousand people died.

The beautiful documentary, *Coda*, features the life of Ryuichi Sakamoto, one of Japan's most famous and successful artists. Sakamoto is obsessed with sound. As a singer, songwriter, actor, and activist, he has created beautiful sounds for over four decades, garnering numerous awards including an Oscar, a

Grammy, and two Golden Globes. The film follows his journeys to various continents as he discovers and records various sounds, both natural and man-made. He learns of a piano that miraculously survived the tsunami, floated amidst the flood waters, and then rested on the stage of the Miyagi High School of Agriculture. He travels to northeast Japan to see this piano. He walks up on the stage and approaches the piano slowly and reverently. He sees the indelible watermarks left by the flood and observes where the piano has been warped, frayed, and left out of tune. Sakamoto states, "I want to hear if a sound can still come from it." He sits down, strikes each key, leans back patiently, and listens to each sound. Despite its damage, the master still believes it can bring forth beautiful music. Despite the damage the instrument has suffered, Sakamoto is pleased with its sound. [1]

Leading in the midst of brokenness and wounds can be exhausting. It can feel overwhelming and, at times, seem downright impossible. We are tempted to believe we have nothing to offer in our warped and frayed existence. But the kinds of leaders needed in our new reality are ones gripped by a vision of a compassionate God who wants to heal – the One who travels long distances to climb the steps, who still longs to hear what sound can come out of our broken and out of tune pianos. [2]

Leadership is learning to manage tension healthily. A leader is someone who builds trust, bears pain, and gives hope. No matter who you are, where you live, how old you may be or what organization, business, church, or team you are a part of, if you *build trust, bear pain, and give hope, you are a leader*. Which means leadership and healing are inextricably linked together.

Trust and relationship are the lifeblood of leadership, more so now than ever before. With so much uncertainty in our world, trust is not just a good idea; it's absolutely required. The level of our leadership will be determined by the depth of our trust.

And trust is built most significantly in times of healing and pain. We build trust with others when we see them for who they are, when we give others a full-bodied yes with our presence, when we communicate clearly – and only sometimes with our words. When people feel alone and vulnerable, when they wonder if they will ever get out of their pain, when they doubt if anyone will truly know them for who they really are—this is when they need people to show up for them. Trust is built when people pay attention, take notice, and exhibit care and compassion.

There are enticing temptations, however, which lurk around leaders, even Christian leaders. More specifically, Nouwen writes that there are the three alluring temptations: to be relevant, to be spectacular, and to be powerful.[3] They are always present. When people are suffering, we can be tempted to be the one who attempts to fix their problems, and thus we become relevant, spectacular, and powerful all at once. But that is not our role. We are called to be present with people – to bring our full selves to those we are called to lead. Yet, if all we did was sit with people in their pain and agony, they could easily become overwhelmed by the seemingly unbearable weight of the pain. It's why we must also *give hope*. If we bear pain (and thus, build trust with others) but there is no hope to offer, it can lead to a deep sense of cynicism and despair. The world is looking for people who offer hope. But grief is not the same as despair. One can grieve with hope, but hopeless grief leads to despondency.

Bear pain, build trust, give hope. If we only live in one realm, we are unhelpful. If we live in two of three, we usher in a flimsy view of the future. But when leaders build trust, bear pain, and give hope – *this* is what a wounded world looks for.

We must be *hopeful and expectant* as well as *realistic and prepared*. If leaders remain hopeful and expectant that God is at work and is still on the throne in the midst of suffering, yet they fail to acknowledge the pain and the messiness, we miss the mark. Yes, God is still in control and on the throne; while it sounds comforting on the surface, it can be received as pithy and limp, leaving others with little substance.

Other leaders live in the reality of pain and suffering in our world, but their anxious presence and frenetic activity stunt their ability to carry any expectation about a hopeful future. These leaders are marked by an immense amount of fear and worry as they seek to control the uncontrollable. They leave the world with little vision for what a hope in the God of the Universe looks like in uncertain times. We must find the delicate yet necessary balance of hope and realism. Paul articulated living in this tension by saying they were "hard pressed on every side, but not crushed; perplexed, but not in despair; persecuted, but not abandoned; struck down, but not destroyed" (2 Cor. 4:8-9). And he continued in this hopeful realism and realistic hope: "Therefore we do not lose heart. Though outwardly we are wasting away, yet inwardly we are being renewed day by day. For our light and momentary troubles are achieving for us an eternal glory that far outweighs them all" (vv. 16-17).

To live in this tension, leaders must possess *wisdom, courage,* and *compassion.* For leaders to live in only one or two of these circles will not do. Wisdom and compassion – but without courage – is riskless. We fail to possess courage, to step out, to take risks as bringers of healing. Compassion and courage – but without wisdom – is reckless. We may be well-intentioned and full of zeal, but without wisdom we can cause great damage. And wisdom and courage – but without compassion – is careless.[4] As Paul reminds us, "If I have the gift of prophecy and can fathom all mysteries and all knowledge, and if I have faith that can move mountains, but do not have love, I am nothing" (1 Cor. 13:2). But when leaders possess wisdom, courage, and compassion in equal measures it is priceless.

Bringers of healing, the kinds of leaders we need to help lead off the map, must learn to live in the tensions. Build trust, bear pain, and also give hope. We are hopeful and expectant and also realistic and ready. We possess wisdom, compassion, and also courage.

Leading in the Way of the Wounded Healer

Christian leadership is far from easy. In fact, it is messy, costly, complex, and agonizing. It cracks us open and leaves us exposed. Sometimes it feels as though leadership is the most wounding of all callings. And if we do not deal with the wounds of leadership appropriately, it can damage others significantly. So, what does this mean to pay attention to our inner world as leaders who desire to be bringers of healing?

First, we must readily acknowledge that much will have to die in us for us to be made whole.

When we are leaders, sometimes picking up our cross can feel heavier than for others. Mark Sayers wrote that Christian leadership is learning to die in public. This death-in-public reality involves both joy and searing pain, elation and immense disappointment, lament and celebration. To be leaders who heal and healers who lead, we must die to our own preferences, to our longings for control, to our need to have things done our way, to our desire to have our motives understood correctly. Reading that last sentence may make many leaders wonder why anyone would pursue leadership at all. As leaders, we are used to setting the agenda, but in order for others (and ourselves!) to heal, we must let go of outcomes. This can be excruciating.

Second, we must expect to be misunderstood.

Few things are as painful for leaders as being misunderstood. Decisions are critiqued. Motives are called into question. The emotionally immature get all the airtime. Malicious rumors circulate with lightning speed. The naysayers stir up contention.

The dissenters call for your head on a platter. Especially in times where uncertainty, stress, and anxiety are high, people are often prone to act unhealthily and often assume the worst in us. As the adage goes, hurt people hurt people. Admittedly, there are times as a leader where I simply want to stand up and say, *I am doing the best I can. I cannot please you all! Can you give me a break for just one week? I'm trying to help you, not hurt you. Can't you see that?* Of course, I can't verbalize this, although there have been many times I have wanted to.

When we as leaders read about the wilderness journey of the Israelites in the book of Exodus, don't we feel some sympathy for Moses? Can't we relate to his pain, impatience, and loneliness? Can't we sympathize with many of his complaints directed at God? Such is leadership. As leaders, we seek to pursue the truth and help lead others toward healing and wholeness. And yet those we lead often long to believe their own truth in certain situations. Sometimes it's driven by fear or worry or baggage from their own heartbreaking experience; other times, it is out of arrogance, immaturity, impatience, or a desire to control. Regardless of the motive, it scorches our hearts with the hiss of a scalding cattle prod.

Jesus knew what it meant to be misunderstood as a leader. Riding into Jerusalem on a donkey, many envisioned him as the military hero they had been waiting for all these years, one who would overthrow the oppressive Roman government. *Hosannas* and palm branches – and within a week's time, the people turned on him. Hung on a cross with a sign over his head: *King of the Jews.* Mocked by Roman soldiers and the thieves hanging on either side of him. Scorned by the religious leaders who snarled, "He saved others, but he can't save himself! He's the king of Israel! Let him come down now from the cross, and we will believe in him" (Mt. 27:42). And Jesus could have responded, raging with the largest of let-me-tell-you-something-about-power response in human history. *Yet instead, he willfully chose to remain silent and remain on the cross.*

Even as Jesus physically healed many people, he purposefully and, at times adamantly, instructed others *not* to tell anyone what he had done—what scholars call the messianic secret. Yet the newly healed and restored were often quickly disobedient, sharing with anyone who might listen how they had experienced healing. (To be fair, I'm not sure I'd be able to keep my life-altering encounter to myself either.) Healing work, even healing leadership, is meaningful, but it can still be lonely, underappreciated, and grossly misunderstood. But we still must remain faithful to our calling as bearers of wounds and bringers of healing in Jesus' name.

And third, we must come to expect sabotage.

Leadership is not just about being misunderstood. It's much worse than that. As Edwin Friedman wrote, leaders should expect sabotage.[5] Leadership really isn't leadership until someone calls for your head. The threats are verbalized. The ultimatum is given. Your biggest supporter, who cared for you when others wounded you, has now turned on you and left shrapnel deeply embedded in your own heart. We might be able to handle the Peters who deny us out of fear, but when the Judases who willfully plan to betray us are in our midst, leadership can seem overwhelming. We want to be wounded healers, but now we're just left wounded and in need of healing altogether. Sometimes it feels as if there isn't enough money in the account to pay a therapist for the time needed to help us work through these kinds of scenarios. And yet, amazingly, Jesus willfully and joyfully washed both Peter's and Judas' feet – *even with the full and complete knowledge of what each of them would do to him shortly thereafter.* Leadership is washing the feet of Peter and Judas with the knowledge of what will soon follow. Leadership is voluntarily signing up to be wounded.

We wonder if maybe we should be in some other field, if we should quit our ministry role, resign from leadership, and drive a truck for UPS. We check online job boards and brush up our resume. Yet something says to stay in it. We keep absorbing the pain and wondering how much more we can take. It is beyond humility; now we are with the territory of humiliation. What now? All of this misunderstanding and sabotage require such deep faith and immense amounts of hope and patience. It is no wonder the King James Version translates the word patience with the archaic word *longsuffering*. A longsuffering person shows immense restraint and refuses to seek out revenge. It is patience mixed with merciful hope. Longsuffering is a part of the nature of God, the character of Jesus, and thus, the character of his followers, especially those followers called to lead others. Which means, at times it is excruciating when we have to suffer long with others who are hurting – even those who are hurting us, purposefully or unintentionally. We are called to keep hope and extend grace – to others and ourselves.

We know we will be wounded as we try to lead others to healing. Is it worth it? Yes. Yes, it is. We may not see it on paper. As we look around, we may find scant evidence it's worthwhile. But it's there. This is why leadership requires so much of our trust. When we see leadership as a way to extend the gift of healing to our wounded world, we offer others a glimpse of the future which helps them make sense of their past by sharing Jesus with them in the present. For he is our wounded healer, the one who "heals the brokenhearted and binds up their wounds" (Ps. 147:3). In order to lead others toward healing, we oftentimes must experience the wounds from the very people we are serving. It's painful – excruciating, even – but it's worth it because we are not alone. Our God is a God of healing.

What sound might the master still desire to play when he lays his fingers on the keys of the warped piano?

Conclusion

The Importance of Connection

On the wall of my office hangs a framed print titled *Christ and Abbot Mena.* The eighth century Coptic wooden icon comes from the monastery of Bawit in central Egypt, but now resides in the Louvre in Paris. Despite a few cracks, it is in relatively good condition – especially considering it is the oldest known Coptic icon created over a millennium ago. In the icon, Jesus stands side by side with Abbot Mena, the superior of the Bawit monastery, with his arm around Mena's shoulder. It is a posture of warm friendship and protection. I'm not normally one smitten by ancient icons, but this image always moves me. Each time I look at it hanging on my office wall, I receive it as an invitation to be a friend of Jesus and a challenge to deepen my trust in him.

The world is disconnected, longing and groaning to be restored back to *shalom.* If you find yourself longing to join with Jesus in the healing process, but still unsure how or where to start, let me encourage you with this: *just connect.* God has created us for connection. He hardwired it right into our emotional, mental, physical, and spiritual circuit board. God has created in each human being the desire to be seen, to be known, to be pursued, and to be delighted in. We don't just want others' presence; we *need* it. We are conditioned for connection.[1] Throughout this book, we've explored how we all need healing. We looked at trauma as the experience of disconnection. Thus, the reversal of trauma – the process of healing – can only occur through connection.

Physical healing occurs when the cells, neurons, bones, muscles, ligaments, and tissues begin to connect to one another again, functioning in their original state. Emotional and relational healing occurs when reconnection is established through forgiveness, reconciliation, trust, safety, redemption, and love.

Spiritual healing occurs when we reconnect back to our original design – to the heart of our loving Father – a place of true freedom, hope, and peace. Healing is always about connection.

Jesus, the God who dressed in human flesh and came to be among the people he created, puts his wounded arm around us to comfort us, to befriend us, to remind us we are not alone, and to ask us to trust his wounds for the sake of our own healing. And as we trust him with our wounds, he invites us to join with him to be bringers of healing to others in his name.

Truly, this is what the world is looking for.

Acknowledgments

Writing is an act of paradox; it is most often done in isolation, and yet it is always a team sport. Many people partnered with me throughout the writing process – several deserving specific mention.

Thanks to Chris Backert, who believed the message of this book needed to be shared with the world.

Thanks to Ryan Tate for his creative design work on this project, among many others.

Thanks to my Team of Readers who patiently read through versions of the manuscript and provided honest, valuable, and specific feedback on a short timeline: Lindsay Smith, Ben Pitzen, Dave Briggs, April Karli, Paul Hill, Janet Durrwachter, Caleb Mangum, Peter Gowesky, Rob Chifokoyo, Doug Walker, and Brandon Morrow. This book is better because of you.

A special thanks to Dr. Phil Monroe whose expertise on the topic of the Christian response to trauma was invaluable. His teachings, interviews, conversations, and online training materials were deeply formative and clarifying in the writing process.

Thanks to Dr. Leonard Sweet whose thoughts in the spring of 2020 helped me to clarify the sacred call for the church to be healers in the midst of the pandemic and beyond.

Thanks to Keisha Polonio, whose ongoing thoughts and conversations about trauma, woundedness, hope, and the way of Jesus have pushed me to think more deeply and live more faithfully.

Thanks to my editor, Jason Krell, for his insightful perspective, helpful suggestions, and sage recommendations. You've made this a better message. And thanks to Julie Castro for keeping us on track and on time.

Thanks to the Fresh Expressions U.S. team for being such a joy to serve alongside of. You not only teach others to be resilient, faithful, creative, expectant, compassionate, courageous, and hopeful; you live and lead that way, too.

Thanks to my wife, Megan, and my two sons, Carter and Bennett, for your ongoing encouragement, patience, and understanding as I wrote during such a turbulent and intense season of our lives.

And thank you to Jesus, our Wounded Healer, who, despite our weaknesses and limitations, graciously invites us into his mission of saving and healing, which is available for all creation.

All is grace.

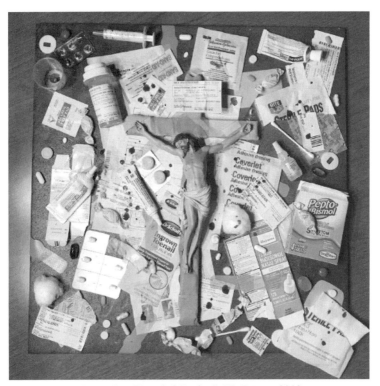

"Jesus, Our Wounded Healer," J.R. Briggs, 2019.

Yet it was our sicknesses he carried;
   it was our diseases that weighed him down.
And we thought his troubles were a punishment from God,
   a punishment for his own sins!
But he was pierced for our rebellion,
   crushed for our sins.
He was beaten so we could be whole.
   He was whipped so we could be healed.

   —ISAIAH 53:4-5

Recommended Resources

Books
- *The Wounded Healer* (Henri Nouwen)
- *A Grief Observed* (C.S. Lewis)
- *Together: The Healing Power of Human Connection in a Sometimes Lonely World* (Vivek Murthy)
- *Handle with Care: How Jesus Redeems the Power of Touch in Life and Ministry* (Lore Ferguson Wilbert)
- *Christ and Calamity: Grace and Gratitude in the Darkest Valley* (Harold L. Senkbeil)
- *The Care of Souls: Cultivating a Pastor's Heart* (Harold L. Senkbeil)
- *Emotionally Healthy Spirituality: It's Impossible to Be Spiritually Mature While Remaining Emotionally Immature* (Peter Scazzerro)
- *The Emotionally Healthy Church: A Strategy for Discipleship that Actually Changes Lives* (Peter Scazzerro)
- *Fail: Finding Hope and Grace in the Midst of Ministry Failure* (J.R. Briggs)
- *Companions in the Darkness: Seven Saints Who Struggled with Depression and Doubt* (Diana Gruver)
- *The Soul of Shame: Retelling the Stories We Believe About Ourselves* (Curt Thompson)
- *A Church Called Tov: Forming a Goodness Culture*

That Resists Abuses of Power and Promotes Healing (Scot McKnight, Laura Barringer)
- *From Burned Out to Beloved: Soul Care for Wounded Healers* (Bethany Dearborn Hiser)

Trauma
- *Suffering and the Heart of God: How Trauma Destroys and Christ Restores* (Diane Langberg)
- *The Body Keeps the Score* (Besel Vander Kolk)
- *Healing the Wounds of Trauma* (American Bible Society)
- *Joyful Journey: Listening to Immanuel* (Wilder, Kang, Loppnow, Loppnow)
- *A Walking Disaster: What Surviving Katrina and Cancer Taught Me About Faith and Resilience* (Jamie Aten)

Mental Health and the Church
- *Grace for the Afflicted: A Clinical and Biblical Perspective on Mental Illness* (Matthew S. Stanford)
- *Troubled Minds: Mental Illness and the Church's Mission* (Amy Simpson)
- *The Pastoral Handbook of Mental Illness: A Guide for Training and Reference* (Steve Bloem)
- *Spurgeon's Sorrows: Realistic Hope for those who Suffer from Depression* (Zack Eswine)
- *Finding Quiet: My Story of Overcoming Anxiety and the Practices that Brought Peace* (J.P. Moreland)

The Holy Spirit
- *Everybody Gets to Play* (John Wimber)
- *Miracle Work: A Down-to-Earth Guide to Supernatural Ministries* (Jordan Seng)
- *Surprised by the Power of the Spirit* (Jack Deere)

Leadership
- *Canoeing the Mountains: Christian Leadership in Uncharted Territory* (Tod Bolsinger)
- *A Tale of Three Kings: A Study in Brokenness* (Gene Edwards)
- *The Vulnerable Pastor* (Mandy Smith)
- *Managing Leadership Anxiety: Yours and Theirs* (Steve Cuss)
- *The Imperfect Pastor* (Zack Eskwine)
- *Leading With a Limp: Take Full Advantage of your Most Powerful Weakness* (Dan Allender)
- *Contextual Intelligence: Unlocking the Ancient Secret to Mission on the Front Lines* (Leonard Sweet and Michael Adam Beck)

History of Healing in Christianity
- *The Rise of Christianity* (Rodney Stark)
- *Healing in the History of Christianity* (Amanda Porterfield)
- *Medicine and Health Care in Early Christianity* (Gary B. Ferngren)

Websites
- Trauma Healing Institute at American Bible Society: www.traumahealinginstitute.org
- Humanitarian Disaster Institute: https://www.wheaton.edu/academics/academic-centers/humanitarian-disaster-institute/
- Churches That Heal: www.churchesthatheal.com (Dr. Henry Cloud)
- Tony Cauchi, "The Healing Ministry of Jesus in the Gospels." November 2011 http://voiceofhealing.info/01_history/gospels.html
- COVID-19 Spiritual First Aid by the Humanitarian Disaster Institute (free PDF download): https://www.wheaton.edu/media/humanitarian-disaster-institute/COVID-19-spiritual-first-aid-tip-sheet.pdf
- www.freshexpressionsus.org

Endnotes

Chapter 1

1. "Pope Francis' Homily: The Church Should Be Like a Field Hospital," Rome Reports, February 5, 2015, https://www.romereports.com/en/2015/02/05/pope-francis-homily-the-church-should-be-like-a-field-hospital/.

2. "US Deaths in 2020 Top 3 Million, by Far Most Ever Counted." Associated Press, 22 Dec. 2020, https://apnews.com/article/us-coronavirus-deaths-top-3-million-e2bc856b6ec45563b84ee2e87ae8d5e7. Accessed 23 Dec. 2020.

3. Ibid.

4. Woefully shortsighted, many thought a national shortage of toilet paper would be one of the most significant setbacks we would face.

5. Amanda Jackson, "A Crisis Mental-Health Hotline Has Seen an 891% Spike in Calls," CNN.com, April 10, 2020, https://www.cnn.com/2020/04/10/us/disaster-hotline-call-increase-wellness-trnd/index.html.

6. "3 Times More Women Killed by Men Than Average During U.K. Coronavirus Lockdown," CBS News, April 16, 2020, https://www.cbsnews.com/video/3-times-more-women-killed-by-men-than-average-during-u-k-coronavirus-lockdown/?ftag=CNM-00-10aac3a.

7. https://www.espn.com/nba/story/_/id/30719214/minnesota-timberwolves-karl-anthony-towns-says-tested-positive-covid-19.

8   Kate Shellnutt, "2020's Most-Read Bible Verse: 'Do Not Fear,'" Christianity Today, December 3, 2020, https://www.christianitytoday.com/news/2020/december/most-popular-verse-youversion-app-bible-gateway-fear-covid.html.

9   Other attacks have been made on the U.S. Capitol building in our history, including the British who burned the building in 1814 during the War of 1812, Puerto Rican nationalists who opened fired on the floor of the house in 1954, and far-left extremists who detonated a bomb in the Senate chamber in 1983. https://www.smithsonianmag.com/smart-news/history-violent-attacks-capitol-180976704/.

10 https://www.cnn.com/2021/01/19/politics/biden-covid-victims-memorial/index.html.

11 See Bolsinger's book *Canoeing the Mountains: Christian Leadership in Uncharted Territory* (Downers Grove, IL: InterVarsity Press, 2018).

12 Many have used the language "the new normal." I don't believe this has been helpful. Instead, I've embraced the language of "the new reality" (and, at times, "the new abnormal").

13 Christopher J.H. Wright, *The Mission of God* (Downers Grove, IL: InterVarsity Press, 2006), 62.

14 Jordan Seng, *Miracle Work: A Down-to-Earth Guide to Supernatural Ministries* (Downers Grove, IL: InterVarsity Press, 2013), 82.

15 Jordan Seng, *Miracle Work: A Down-to-Earth Guide to Supernatural Ministries* (Downers Grove, IL: InterVarsity Press, 2013), 85.

16 Mr. Rogers, "Fred Rogers: Look for the Helpers," YouTube: https://www.youtube.com/watch?v=-LGHtc_D328.

Chapter 2

1 Henri Nouwen, *The Wounded Healer*, 93.

2 Atul Gawande, *Being Mortal: Medicine and What Matters in the End* (Metropolitan Books: New York, 2014), 8-9.

3 "Coronavirus & Quarantine: Lament, Hope and Creativity Edition" (Webinar 3), The Veritas Forum, April 13, 2020, http://www.veritas.org/veritasforumlivestream3/.

4 On the surface, this story can seem deeply disturbing and raises many unsettling questions for some people. Additional context, time, and space is needed to unpack all the implications of this story in its fullness.

5 Consider how counterintuitive this must have felt for the Israelites. The snakes represented poison, evil, and death. And yet, they experienced healing when they looked at a snake on a pole.

6 In 2 Kings 18:1-4, we read that seven hundred years later, the Israelites brought the pole into the Promised Land. King Hezekiah, who "did what was right in the sight of the Lord," destroyed it because the people had named it Nehushtan and were worshiping it.

7 For a beautiful portrayal of the biblical stories in Numbers 21 and John 3, watch the episode "Invitations" (Season 1, Episode 7), *The Chosen*, directed by Dallas Jenkins. March 2020.

8   Christopher Eames, "Does the Serpentine Symbol of Healing Have a Biblical Origin?" Watch Jerusalem, February 15, 2019, https://watchjerusalem.co.il/540-does-the-serpentine-symbol-of-healing-have-a-biblical-origin.

9   "The Rod of Asclepius and Caduceus: Two Ancient Symbols," Florence Inferno, updated June 27, 2016, https://www.florenceinferno.com/rod-of-asclepius-and-caduceus-symbols/.

10 Gary B. Ferngren, *Medicine and Health Care in Early Christianity*. (Baltimore: Johns Hopkins University Press, 2009), 137.

11 Eames, "Does the Serpentine Symbol of Healing Have a Biblical Origin?"

12 Also see Exodus 4:1-5 and 7:8-12 about other stories of Moses interacting with snakes.

13 John Mark Comer, *The Ruthless Elimination of Hurry: How to Stay Emotionally Healthy and Spiritually Alive in the Chaos of the Modern World*, (Colorado Springs, CO: Waterbrook Press, 2019), 77.

14 Through this lens, if you read the story of blind Bartimaeus in Mark 10:46-52 it becomes more textured. When Bartimaeus shouts, "Jesus, Son of David, have mercy on me!" he is acknowledging that he believes Jesus can heal him. In Jewish tradition, the term Son of David implied that Jesus had healing powers (Josephus, Antiquities, 8.2.5 [8:42-49]). Despite his blindness, it seems Bartimaeus was able to see well enough to recognize the sozo reality of Jesus.

15 Jordan Seng, *Miracle Work: A Down-to-Earth Guide to Supernatural Ministries* (Downers Grove, IL: InterVarsity Press, 2013), 85.

16 Mk. 5:23; Lk. 8:36; Lk. 6:17-19; Acts 3:1-10

17 Nouwen, *The Wounded Healer*, 82.

18 Ibid, 94.

19 Ibid, 100.

20 Ibid, 94.

21 For more on Wabi-Sabi, see my previous book *Fail: Finding Hope in the Midst of Ministry Failure*, pp. 148-149.

22 "Coronavirus & Quarantine: Lament, Hope and Creativity Edition"

Chapter 3

1 Tony Cauchi, "The Healing Ministry of Jesus in the Gospels," *The Voice of Healing*, November 2011, http://voiceofhealing.info/01_history/gospels.html.

2 Amanda Porterfield, *Healing in the History of Christianity* (Oxford, Oxford University Press, 2005), 21.

3 Ibid, 21.

4 Gary B. Ferngren, *Medicine and Health Care in Early Christianity*. (Baltimore: Johns Hopkins University Press, 2009), 46.

5 Amanda Porterfield, *Healing in the History of Christianity* (Oxford, Oxford University Press, 2005), 32.

6 Ibid, 21.

7 Cauchi, "The Healing Ministry of Jesus in the Gospels."

8 Lv. 13:45; Nm. 5:2

9   See Lev. 13; 2 Kgs. 5; Lk. 5:12-14, 17:11-19; Mt. 26:6; Mk. 1:40-45

10   Even Paul was given power by God to heal in Acts 19:11-12. Even the handkerchiefs and aprons Paul touched were placed on sick people and they were healed!

11   John Wimber, "Signs and Wonders in the Gospels, Acts and Letters," Signs and Wonders Conference, London, England, 1984.

12   First appeared on Christianity Today's website: "Our Personal Scars Can Help Others Heal" on September 24, 2020: https://www.christianitytoday.com/ct/2020/september-web-only/briggs-nouwen-scars-help-others-heal-wounded-healers.html.

13   Christopher J.H. Wright, *Knowing Jesus through the Old Testament* (Second Edition), Downers Grove, IL: InterVarsity Press, 2014), 254-255.

Chapter 4

1   "Anthony Jeselnik, Thoughts and Prayers – Virtue Signaling on Social Media," YouTube, November 13, 2015, https://www.youtube.com/watch?v=PTmCxbcRXs4.

2   Shane Claiborne interview on Guy Kawasaki's Remarkable People podcast, March 18, 2020.

3   Sarah K. Yeomans, "Pandemics in Perspective," *Biblical Archaeology Review*, Fall 2020, pp. 18-19.

4   Ibid.

5   Chris Gehrz, "Courage and Pestilence," *Christian History Magazine*; Issue 135, (Worcester, PA: Christian History Institute, 2020), 24.

6   Ibid.

7   "Plague and Epidemic Throughout History," *Christian History Magazine*, Issue 135, (Worcester, PA: Christian History Institute, 2020), 22-23.

8   Gary B. Ferngren, *Medicine and Health Care in Early Christianity*, (Baltimore: Johns Hopkins University Press, 2009), 30.

9   Harold L. Senkbeil, *The Care of Souls: Cultivating a Pastor's Heart*, (Lexham Press, 2019), 33.

10 Eusebius, *Ecclesiastical History*, 9.8.

11 Amanda Porterfield, *Healing in the History of Christianity*, (Oxford, Oxford University Press, 2005), 52.

12 Edwin Woodruff Tait, "Our Scattered Leaves," *Christian History Magazine*; Issue 135, (Worcester, PA: Christian History Institute, 2020), 40.

13 Rodney Stark, *The Rise of Christianity: How the Obscure, Marginal Jesus Movement Became the Dominant Religious Force in the Western World in a Few Centuries,* (HarperSanFrancisco, 1997), 161.

14 Gary B. Ferngren, *Medicine and Health Care in Early Christianity*. (Baltimore: Johns Hopkins University Press, 2009), 118.

15 Ibid.

16 Martin Luther, *Luther's Works*, Vol. 43: Devotional Writings II, ed Jaroslav Jan Pelikan, Hilton C, Oswald, and Helmut T, Lehmann, vol 43 (Philadelphia: Fortress Press, 1999), 119-138.

17 Luther, 124.

18 Dan Graves, "Buried Alive: Father Damien Chose to Serve Lepers for Christ," *Christian History Magazine*; Issue 135, (Worcester, PA: Christian History Institute, 2020), 35.

19 For a wonderful book on the story of Father Damien, read *Leper Priest of Moloka'i: The Father Damien Story* written by Richard Stewart (Honolulu, HI: University of Hawaii Press, 2000).

20 Ibid.

21 "Notre-Dame De Paris, A Place of Healing," *Friends of Notre-Dame De Paris*, May, 18, 2020, https://www.friendsofnotredamedeparis.org/news/notre-dame-de-paris-a-place-of-healing.

22 Tomás Halík, "Christianity in a Time of Sickness," American Magazine, April 3, 2020, https://www.americamagazine.org/faith/2020/04/03/christianity-time-sickness?fbclid=IwAR17iEzxsl8ZFOvPXGP-0pk0biNZz5SA_41Gw7WDWdEXFgfYNl97gmr_N9HA.

23 Dr. Phil Monroe, Fresh Expressions U.S. Resilient Church Academy: Trauma Healing Academy Track webinar, August 19, 2020.

24 E. James Wilder, Anna Kang, John Loppnow, Sungshim Loppnow. *Joyful Journey: Listening to Immanuel* (Los Angeles: Presence and Practice, 2015), 26.

25 Elissa Melaragno, "Trauma in the Body: An Interview with Dr. Bessel van der Kolk," August 13, 2020, http://www.dailygood.org/story/1901/trauma-in-the-body-an-interview-with-dr-bessel-van-der-kolk/.

26 A wonderful resource seeking to equip churches to help

27 Dr. Phil Monroe, Fresh Expressions U.S. Resilient Church Academy: Trauma Healing Academy Track webinar, August 19, 2020.

28 In the story of Numbers 21 we looked at earlier, it is interesting God doesn't just heal the people, nor does He erect the bronze snake on a wooden pole. Instead, he asks Moses to craft the snake and erect it – and then healing occurs. He invited Moses to join him in the healing process. Without God, there would be no healing, but without Moses, there would have been nothing to look to for that healing.

29 Dr. Phil Monroe, Fresh Expressions U.S. Resilient Church Academy: Trauma Healing Academy Track online webinar, August 26, 2020.

30 Frederick Buechner, *Whistling in the Dark: A Doubter's Dictionary* (San Francisco, HarperOne, 1993), 117.

31 Paul writes to the church in Ephesus that the purpose of the church is to equip God's people for good works of service in the name of Jesus for the good of the world (Eph. 4:12-16).

32 To learn more about the mission and work of COSILoveYou visit www.COSILoveYou.com.

33 Interview on the Monday Morning Pastor podcast, May 2020, https://podcasts.apple.com/us/podcast/monday-morning-pastor/id1455648175.

34 See http://thi.americanbible.org/ for more information on the Trauma Healing Institute.

Chapter 5

1. See chapter 6 "Being Peculiar" in my book *The Sacred Overlap: Learning To Live Faithfully in the Space Between* (Grand Rapids, MI: Zondervan, 2020) for more on the important work of the Holy Spirit and how we can learn to trust the Spirit more fully.

2. Amanda Porterfield, *Healing in the History of Christianity* (Oxford, Oxford University Press, 2005), 173.

3. Philip Jenkins, "Epidemics: How the Church Has Responded Through History", March 2020, Fresh Expressions Webinar, www.freshexpressionsus.org.

4. Amanda Porterfield, *Healing in the History of Christianity* (Oxford, Oxford University Press, 2005), 174.

5. Harold Senkbeil, *The Care of Souls: Cultivating a Pastor's Heart* (Lexham Press, 2019), 153.

6. Posted on Rich Villodas' Facebook page, Pentecost Sunday, May 31, 2020.

7. See Wimber's book *Everyone Gets to Play* (Garden City, ID: Ampelon Publishing, 2009).

8. Wayne Grudem, *Systematic Theology: An Introduction to Biblical Doctrine* (Grand Rapids, MI: Zondervan, 1994), 634.

9. Is. 32:14-18, 44:3

10. Ps. 104:30; Jb. 34:14-15; Jn. 6:63

11. Acts 1:8; 1 Cor. 12:11

12. 1 Cor. 6:11; Ti. 3:5

13. Acts 15:28

14. See Wayne Grudem's *Systematic Theology: An Introduc-

tion to Biblical Doctrine (Grand Rapids, MI: Zondervan, 1994), pp. 635-646.

15 Ibid, 1064.

16 For more on the baptism of the Holy Spirit see Mt. 3:11; Mk. 1:8; Lk. 3:16, 24:49; Jn. 1:33; Acts 1:5,8, 11:16; and 1 Cor. 12:13.

17 Jordan Seng defined baptism of the Holy Spirit this way: "An empowering manifestation of God's indwelling presence in an individual. The baptism involves the Spirit manifesting in an individual with such intensity that supernatural things tend to occur in that moment – most notably the expression of spiritual gifts such as tongues or prophecy... Believers typically don't receive the baptism of the Spirit until they attend to it directly, and having received it they can certainly seek repeated dousing of the spirits presence and power." Jordan Seng, *Miracle Work: A Down-to-Earth Guide to Supernatural Ministries*, (Downers Grove, IL: InterVarsity Press, 2013), 191.

18 Grudem, 765.

19 Ibid, 782.

20 Lk. 4:40

21 Mk. 6:13; Jas. 5:14-15

22 1 Cor. 7:7, 12:8-10, 28; Eph. 4:11; Rom. 12:6-8; 1 Pt. 4:11

23 Grudem, 1067.

Chapter 6

1 Ernest Hemingway, *The Fifth Column and the First Forty-Nine Stories* (New York: Charles Scribern's Sons, 1938).

2   While not everyone has embraced the wearing of masks, generally the American public has understood its importance for safety and health reasons. Please don't read this as a political statement about masks; I am sharing this merely for journalistic perspective.

3   COVID-19 is, of course, a respiratory disease, which involves symptoms of shortness of breath. It evokes the biblical words for wind and breath (*ruach* in Hebrew, *pneuma* in Greek), which also means spirit. From this, we get our word *pneumonia*.

4   Ibid, 174.

5   Ibid.

6   "Resilience," Center on the Developing Child, Harvard University, https://developingchild.harvard.edu/science/key-concepts/resilience.

7   Yuval Levin, *A Time to Build: From Family and Community to Congress and the Campus, How Recommitting To Our Institutions Can Revive the American Dream* (New York: Basic Books, 2020), 123.

8   The Rev. Kendall Palladino, "Mother Teresa Saw Loneliness as Leprosy of the West," *News-Times*, updated November 16, 2009, https://www.newstimes.com/news/article/Mother-Teresa-saw-loneliness-as-leprosy-of-the-250607.php.

9   How bad is it? According to the 2018 report by Henry J. Kaiser Family Foundation, 22 percent of all adults in the U.S. reported they often or always feel lonely or socially isolated—that's well over 55 million people – far more than the number of adult cigarette smokers and nearly double the number of people with diabetes. See Vivek

Murthy's book *Together: The Healing Power of Human Connection in a Sometimes Lonely World* (San Francisco: HarperWave, 2020) for a more thorough treatment of the epidemic of loneliness.

10 Ibid, xix-xx.

11 For more on suicide deaths, see Centers for Disease Control and Prevention, Morbidity and Mortality Weekly Report 67, no. 22, June 8, 2018. For life expectancy see www.cdc.gov/nchs/fastats/life-expectancy.htm.

12 The CDC reported that in 2018 almost seventy thousand Americans died from opioid overdose.

13 Holly Hedegaard, Arialdi M. Minino, and Margaret Warner, Drug Overdose Deaths in the United States, 1999-2017, NCHC Data Brief (Hyattsville, MD: National Center for Health Statistics, 2018), www.cdc.gov/nchs/data/databriefs/db329-h.pdf.

14 Yuval Levin, *A Time to Build: From Family and Community to Congress and the Campus, How Recommitting To Our Institutions Can Revive the American Dream* (New York: Basic Books, 2020), 12.

15 Eric Kleinberg reported that heat waves in the U.S. take more lives in an average year than all other natural disasters combined.

16 See Eric Klinenberg, *Heat Wave: A Social Autopsy of Disaster in Chicago*, Second Edition (Chicago: University of Chicago Press, 2015).

17 Arienne Cohen, "COVID-19 Brings a 'Perfect Storm' of Suicide Risk Factors: Economic Stress, Isolation, Gun Sales," *Fast Company Magazine*, April

22, 2020, https://www.fastcompany.com/90494070/covid-19-brings-a-perfect-storm-of-suicide-risk-factors-economic-stress-isolation-gun-sales?partner=rss&utm_campaign=rss+fastcompany&utm_content=rss&utm_medium=feed&utm_source=rss.

18 Amanda Jackson, "A Crisis Mental-Health Hotline Has Seen an 891% Spike in Calls," CNN, April 10, 2020, https://www.cnn.com/2020/04/10/us/disaster-hotline-call-increase-wellness-trnd/index.html.

19 "Mental Health's New Number," November 2, 2020, *TIME Magazine*, 15.

20 See Mt. 4:23 and Mt. 9:35.

Chapter 7

1 I've used the word marks here with great intention, as wounds do, in fact, leave marks on us.

2 Coronavirus & Quarantine: Lament, Hope and Creativity Edition (Webinar 3), The Veritas Forum, April 13, 2020, http://www.veritas.org/veritasforumlivestream3/.

3 In John 9, the disciples asked Jesus, "Who sinned, this man or his parents, that he was born blind?" Jesus' response was, "Neither this man nor his parents sinned, but this happened so that the works of God may be displayed in him…" (vv. 2-3). Jesus' response shows us that a "just have more faith" response in each person with sickness or ailment is unhelpful and inaccurate (and often deeply wounding).

4 See Psalm 73:11-14 in The Message. Psalm 73 is the first expression in Book III in the Psalms. Book III is collection made up largely of psalms of communal lament. The

fresh language of the psalms in The Message can help us grasp the power and the punch of lament in our prayers – especially Psalm 73. Some have described the back-and-forth emotions here as one of the truest expressions of the Christian experience.

5 Donna Harris, founder of Builders + Backers, believes lament is essential for the healthy processing of our grief, loss, and wounds. She describes lament with more depth, a flow of six movements: crying out to God, affirming our trust in God, petitioning God to restore, making additional arguments, expressing rage against loss and injustice, and praising God in assurance of his promises to hear us. For more, see: https://podcast.praxislabs.org/the-redemptive-edge-donna-harris.

6 Harold L. Senkbeil, *The Care of Souls: Cultivating A Pastor's Heart* (Lexham Press, 2019), 83.

7 Ibid, 79.

8 Amanda Porterfield, *Healing in the History of Christianity* (Oxford, Oxford University Press, 2005), 4.

Chapter 8

1 Coda, directed by, Stephen Nomura Schible, (Production Co: NHK, Avrotros, 2018), 101 minutes.

2 A tip of the cap to Jon Tyson for the Sakamoto story, used in his sermon on the Church of the City New York podcast (September 14, 2020, "Fall Vision Sunday").

3 See Nouwen's classic work *In the Name of Jesus: Reflections on Christian Leadership*. It is so rich and full of such wisdom, it should be required yearly reading for every Christian leader.

4   To see more on this, see page 83 of my book *The Sacred Overlap: Learning to Live Faithfully in the Space Between* (Grand Rapids, MI: Zondervan, 2020).

5   Edwin H. Friedman, *A Failure of Nerve: Leadership in the Age of the Quick Fix* (Bethesda, MD: The Edwin Friedman Estate, 1999), 303.

Conclusion

1   Cyd Holsclaw and Geoff Holsclaw, *Does God Really Like Me?: Discovering the God Who Wants to be With Us* (Downers Grove, IL: InterVarsity Press, 2020), 11-13.

About Fresh Expressions

Fresh Expressions is an international movement of missionary disciples cultivating new kinds of church alongside existing congregations to more effectively engage our growing post-Christian society.

We equip Christians to revitalize the church by starting contextual expressions of Christian community among the many segments, neighborhoods, and people groups of society.

A Note from the Author

If you enjoyed *A Time To Heal*, have further questions, or want to interact with me directly, I'd love to hear from you.

J.R. Briggs
jrbriggs@kairospartnerships.org
www.kairospartnerships.org